Let It Be Incomplete

Unlock the Power of Progress by Overcoming Perfectionism and Procrastination with Inspiring Stories and Novel Insights

Table of content:

Chapter 7 – Commit to enjoy the journey

Gratitude:

To Lord Shri Ram, his highest devotee Hanuman ji and to mother of creativity, Maa Saraswati.

To my wife Akriti, who always pushes me to reach my full potential.

To Ayra, my daughter, who inspires me to be childlike again.

To my parents and sister, who are always with me.

Introduction:

Story of Po the Fat Panda

"There are no accidents."

— Master Oogway, *Kung Fu Panda*

Believe in the chain of events that have brought you to this moment. You are now reading this book to find that one thing, that secret recipe, which will take you closer to your truth. Step by step, you will uncover your path to greatness.

We all know that each of us is unique. There is no one-size-fits-all solution to reaching our full potential. But there are ways and methods that, when applied, will guide us on our journey towards greatness, towards living life at our full potential.

Take the story of Po, the fat panda, from the famous movie *Kung Fu Panda*. Po left his father's noodle shop in search of his path to greatness, to find his "Ikigai," to move closer to his truth. He always dreamed of learning Kung Fu and thus joined the martial arts school of Master Shifu.

At the Kung Fu school, Po met five other warriors training to become the Dragon Warrior: the Tiger, the Viper, the Mantis, the Monkey, and the Crane. Unlike the others, Po had no special powers. Disheartened, he returned to his father's noodle shop. Before leaving, he confided in Shifu, believing he wasn't meant for Kung Fu, as he had no special abilities like the others.

Shifu asked Po why he came to the school in the first place and what made him endure the hardships until that point. Po remembered two things:

1. **Desire for Purpose:** He joined Shifu's school because he wanted to escape his purposeless life and discover his true path, to live a life of greatness.

2. **Faith in Shifu:** He believed in Shifu, trusting that Shifu would transform his life and guide him out of his old habits into a life of purpose and fulfilment. He did not want to spend his life selling noodles; he sought something more.

Shifu had reminded Po of his "why." On your path to purpose, finding your "why" and revisiting it daily is crucial, as it keeps you grounded and focused on why you started the journey. Your "why" is your North Star.

Po decided to continue his training, mastering many Kung Fu techniques at a fast pace. He soon faced his first challenge—learning about his past. Po, aware that the noodle shop owner wasn't his real father, wanted to uncover his origins. He was pained by his past, haunted by the unknown, and knew that to become the Dragon Warrior, he needed to heal.

Po sought the peacock, who knew about his parents, and travelled to his village, where he met his real father. Living with him for some time, Po learned that his parents always deeply loved him, especially his mother. This realization healed Po's past wounds, filling him with newfound Vigor and zest for life.

The path to greatness is dynamic and requires continuous learning. Po returned to Shifu, ready to take on the world and become the Dragon Warrior. But there was an imminent threat: the evil Kung Fu master, Tai Lung, was about to attack the Valley of Peace. Po, still doubting his readiness, sought guidance from Master Oogway, the wisest of all.

"I am a fat panda and still not ready as a Dragon Warrior," Po confessed to Oogway.

"You are too concerned with what was and what will be. Remember, yesterday is history, tomorrow is a mystery, but today is a gift. That's why it is called the present," Oogway wisely replies.

Even Shifu, deeply concerned, approached Master Oogway for help.

"But Master Po is not the Dragon Warrior. How will he save the valley from Tai Lung? Please help me, Master," Shifu pleads.

"Let go of the illusion of control. You need to believe in Po. Promise me, Shifu, you will believe," replies Master Oogway.

As Shifu promised, he began to believe that Po, the fat panda, was indeed the Dragon Warrior destined to save the valley. Using his Kung Fu expertise, Shifu retrieved the Dragon Scroll from the dragon's mouth to give it to Po, the prophesied Dragon Warrior.

When Po opened the Dragon Scroll, he found it held no secret recipe to greatness. It was just a plain mirror. All the powers he needed was already inside him—in his belief in himself. Po realized that believing in oneself is the most powerful force of all. It was this simple truth that enabled him to save the valley and become the Dragon Warrior.

Po's journey teaches us that greatness is not about giving up in the face of challenges; it is about finding solutions and. It is about understanding that each of us has a unique path to greatness. *We must use our past to grow, develop, and become wiser rather than let it wound us.* Like Po, we need to march forward with full belief in ourselves, trusting that we will succeed.

Just as Po transformed from an ordinary panda into the Dragon Warrior, each of us has the potential to unlock our greatness and reach our full potential. *Kung Fu Panda* reveals a profound truth: our strength lies in our willingness to believe in ourselves. We need to become our best friends and our biggest supporters and believe in our success before anyone else.

As Master Oogway wisely tells Shifu, *"Let go of the illusion of control. You need to believe in Po."*

As you read this book, trust your path. Treat this book as a friendly guide, and the methods and solutions provided will inspire you to overcome perfectionism and beat procrastination naturally.

So, let go of doubts and fears, and believe in yourself. Your journey to greatness is uniquely yours, and with each step, you are creating your own extraordinary story. Embrace the present moment and let the power of belief guide you to your full potential.

I invite you on this exciting journey of self-discovery and growth. But before we begin, I ask you to do two things:

1. **Leave your fears and doubts behind:** I know it's easier said than done, but start by writing all your fears and doubts in a diary and let them rest there.

2. **Embrace the power of belief:** Start with these powerful affirmations whenever you read this book.

   - " I believe in myself and my capabilities."
   - " I believe in reaching my true potential and in immense possibilities of growth and abundance "

Begin by doing minor tasks you love—eat your favorite food, call a friend, play a sport, or spend time with family. Start with the simple things and do them consistently.

The Journey Behind the Book

In May 2024, my quest for freedom, which I had named Read4Freedom, was at a crossroads. This journey symbolizes my commitment to growth, continuous learning, and living a fulfilling life.

The origins of this journey trace back to 2018. After seven years of dedicated reading, a profound desire to share knowledge as a book aroused within. I wrote a book recounting my experiences during my MBA days at IIM Indore. I began drafting the manuscript in March 2021 and completed the first draft by July 2021. I was making considerable progress and felt confident that I will publish my book soon.

However, life had its plans for me. At the time of me writing the first draft, I was working in Haridwar, a city renowned as a gateway to the divine—a land of Shiva, forests, The Ganges, and abundant nature. I was fervently seeking a transfer to Jaipur, and by some divine grace, I succeeded.

But with this change came a new set of challenges. Not only did I move to a new city, but I also transitioned to a different department within my organization. From working in the LPG department, I shifted to the Aviation department, requiring me to start anew. Overwhelmed by these changes, my journey with Read4Freedom faltered.

Time passed, and in April 2024 I found myself transferred once again, this time to a remote location in Barmer, in the

Thar desert of Western Rajasthan. I had entrusted my draft to a professional editor, but progress stalled, and I found myself stuck with the draft for six months. Doubts and frustrations crept in, and there were moments when I questioned the worth of continuing with the book.

Despite these setbacks, I remained determined. Reflecting on my childhood, where simplicity and dedication helped me achieve my goals, I continued to persevere. I prayed to Lord Hanuman, seeking courage and wisdom, and to Goddess Saraswati, the Supreme Goddess of creativity.

One day, after playing tennis, I went swimming, and after swimming for sometime I felt deep relaxation, I started meditating while being there in the water and sought a solution for completing my much desired project of the book which I started writing in 2021.

While meditated and prayed in the pool, my prayers were answered. It was then that the idea for a new book, titled *Incomplete*, emerged. This book would address the challenges of perfectionism and procrastination, offering solutions not just for me but for others facing similar struggles.

I let the original first book about my MBA journey be incomplete without worrying much about the effort and time I had put into the project.

Immediately I started writing the book you are reading right now—*let it be incomplete*.

So here you are, holding the result of persistent effort and divine inspiration. I am deeply grateful to Lord Rama, Lord Hanuman, Goddess Saraswati, and the divine creator for guiding me on this journey.

Thank you for joining me on this transformative path. May this book provide you with the insights and inspiration needed to overcome your obstacles and pursue your unique journey of progress.

Why I Am Writing This Book: What You Will Gain

In a world where everyone is racing to be number one, judged by the number of followers on their social media accounts, and constantly measuring their worth by their online presence, we are chasing an endless dream.

In this relentless pursuit, we often forget why we set these goals. While we strive to be the best, more focused, and better than others, we can lose sight of the true meaning of life and the joy of living. We begin to prioritize Instagram followers over genuine friendships and career objectives over family values.

In this pursuit, we can become entangled in a complex emotional web of dream chasing and struggles with incomplete goals, which can be both painful and hindering to our progress. It's essential to recognize that something may be amiss, and we need to correct our course.

I am writing this book to remind you that there is more to life than simply chasing dreams and goals. Learning to enjoy the journey and finding happiness in following the process can be far more rewarding. Realigning our goals with the basics of life can help us lead a more meaningful existence and make us feel more alive.

This book is about moving from obsessing over perfection to choosing progress. It's about transitioning from a stressful pursuit to consciously choosing happiness along the path of excellence and abundance.

Notice that I am not saying that you must not strive for your goals and dreams. All my efforts are in the direction that while you pursue your goals, how you can find happiness in the process of achieving them?

The insights shared in this book have helped me find greater joy while striving to become a world class. I believe that the novel methods and knowledge contained within will not only increase happiness and joy in your life, but also help you achieve your most desirable goals more easily.

While reading this book, you will gain a fresh perspective on achieving your goals in a more joyful and fulfilling way:

1. You will be better *equipped to face your most tough challenges* with powerful strategies to apply whenever you are stuck on your journey.

2. You will be assured that you are *always making progress* in life.

3. You understand that *believing in yourself and taking action as if you cannot fail* is the *holy grail* of success..

4. You will be inspired to pursue your goals with the power of *choosing progress over perfection.*

5. You will move one step closer to your *true potential* and your personal truth.

So, let's begin our journey of choosing progress over perfection.

Chapter 1: Why we get stuck -Understanding the Problem

"If I had an hour to solve a problem, I'd spend 55 minutes thinking about the problem and 5 minutes thinking about solutions." — Albert Einstein

The Deep Pain of being stuck

During my days at IIT, I was naïve about the impact of choosing the right people for friendship. My friend circle included individuals who were experimenting with beer, alcohol, cigarettes, and other substances for fun and adventure. For about a year, I resisted these habits, but by the second year, I found myself falling into the same trap. I began experimenting with harmful substances like beer, alcohol, and cigarettes, thinking it was just part of the adventure.

It's true that you become the sum of the five people you spend the most time with. Unknowingly, I picked up some bad habits from my friend's circle. Despite these challenges, I got into IIM, a prestigious MBA institute. It was my tennis skills and consistent representation of my university at the national level played a significant role in opening those hallowed gates. However, deep down, I knew that my intellectual capabilities had been curtailed by the constant use of these substances.

I have always been someone who loves to compete and succeed in all areas of life—whether in sports, academics, or my career. At IIM, I encountered some of the smartest minds from across India, all competing for the best corporate offers. But my aim at IIM wasn't just about getting a top corporate job; I wanted to enhance my leadership abilities, boost my creativity, and pursue a path of freedom and joy.

However, the reality was much harsher than my imagination. I struggled to sustain the competition and achieve the success I had always been accustomed to. Since childhood, I had set superior standards for myself—if I wasn't in the top five of my class; I considered it a failure. At IIM, I felt like I was losing every day. For someone who was used to winning and excelling in every area, the pain of not meeting expectations was immense.

It was a huge emotional burden. I wanted to run away from IIM, to leave it all behind. I felt completely lost and confused. Instead of seeking help or finding a constructive way forward, I continued to indulge in my bad habits, deteriorating further over the next two years at IIM. Even as I write about those days now, the pain still lingers. I felt alone, disinterested in my courses, and desperate to escape.

Somewhere along the way, I developed a limiting belief: I convinced myself that these habits had affected my memory. As an IIT-IIM graduate with a significant intellectual ego, the idea of diminished cognitive abilities— specifically, a reduced capacity to recall information—was a heavy burden. I obsessed over it for years, researching cures, reading extensively on the subject, and trying various exercises to improve my memory.

I engaged in countless affirmations and began eating almonds, all to overcome this limiting belief. While these actions helped, it wasn't until one afternoon when I was listening to Sadhguru (Indian Yogi & Mystic), that my perspective truly began to shift.

Sadhguru's message was simple yet profound: choose a path, throw yourself into it with all your heart and soul, and you will excel in life. While he was inspiring others to pursue their passions with love and devotion, he said something that struck a chord with me:

"If you remembered a hundred lifetimes of coming up, flying around, falling in love, reproducing, and dying—if you remembered these happenings—would life become meaningless? Because of the loss of memory, everything feels fresh."

Hearing this perspective made me pause. Could my perceived limitation be my greatest strength? How could I transform my biggest challenge into a source of power?

At that moment, I was compelled to start writing this book. Sadhguru's message resonated deeply with me, and I gained a new perspective on memory and its role in our lives. What I once saw as a curse began to feel like a blessing.

This is the core message I want to share with you: it is possible to turn your challenges into strengths. I spent years trapped by the belief that I handled my memory loss because of substance abuse. But now, with this new wisdom, I feel a sense of peace. What once seemed like a significant issue now feels insignificant in the grand scheme of things.

Thank you, Sadhguru, for illuminating my path.

Now, it's time for you to reflect on your own life. What is your major roadblock, and how can you transform that challenge into your strength? Don't waste years feeling stuck, believing there's no way out. My experience, and the experiences of countless others who have faced greater challenges, shows that *there is always a solution.*

Often, our egocentric thinking convinces us that our problems are unique and insurmountable, trapping us in a cage of limiting beliefs. But the path to freedom exists— you just need to acknowledge it, believe in it, and commit to finding your way.

One of the most common mistakes we make is assuming we know it all. This mindset stops us from expanding our knowledge and keeps us trapped in our own thoughts and emotions. To break free, you need to share your struggles with others, exchange knowledge, and open yourself up to new perspectives. It's as simple and profound as that.

Me and my perfectionism

When I began my writing journey, I unconsciously judged my work against my past academic performance, which had consistently yielded the best results. This comparison turned me into the biggest obstacle on my path to progress. However, one thing I did right was to keep reading— relentlessly. I read until I found the solutions that expanded my knowledge base. Along the way, I recognized several mistakes I was making on my writing journey:

a) Constant Comparison: I constantly judged my writing against the best-selling books I was reading, forgetting that the authors of those books had spent 10-15 years honing their craft. This ignorance blinded me to the fact that my journey was just beginning, and such comparisons were premature and unfair.

b) Lack of inspiration: I struggled to stay inspired, focusing too much on the result. Thoughts like, "Who will read my writing? I'm not a world-class writer yet," or

"What's the point of completing this book if no one will read it?" often plagued me. This fixation on the outcome stifled my creativity and motivation.

c) Aiming for Perfection: My goal was to write a world-class book that would inspire readers to improve their lives, to become their best selves, to pursue their dreams, and to find their "ikigai". While this was a noble aim, I was trapped by the limiting belief that "perfection equals excellence." Fortunately, through further reading, I discovered a more empowering thought: "Perfection is just perception; there is perfection in taking consistent imperfect action."

Misconception: Perfectionism is synonymous with high standards and excellence.

Truth: While perfectionists often have high standards, their pursuit of flawlessness can actually hinder performance. The constant fear of making mistakes can lead to procrastination, reduced creativity, and anxiety, ultimately impairing overall performance.

d) Perfectionism and Success: I also believed that perfectionism leads to success. But as I delved deeper into topics like daily improvement and Kaizen, I gained more clarity that it is not perfectionism but daily minor improvements done consistently that lead to success in a holistic way.

Misconception: Being a perfectionist guarantees success and achievement.

Truth: Perfectionism can create a fear of failure that prevents people from taking risks and trying new things. It can lead to chronic dissatisfaction and burnout, making it difficult to experience or sustain long-term success.

e) Perfectionism and Motivation: I held the belief that perfectionists are always highly motivated, which fuelled my drive for perfection.

Misconception: Perfectionists are always highly motivated and driven.

Truth: The intense pressure to meet impossibly high standards can lead to fatigue, frustration, and a lack of motivation. Perfectionists may struggle with low self-esteem and feel demotivated when they perceive themselves as falling short.

f) Perfectionism as a Positive Motivator: I believed that perfectionism was a positive motivator for achieving success, but I later realized how wrong I was.

Misconception: Perfectionism serves as a positive motivator to achieve success.

Truth: While it may seem like a motivator, perfectionism can lead to chronic dissatisfaction and an unhealthy obsession with flawlessness. True motivation comes from setting realistic goals and focusing on personal growth and progress.

Understanding these misconceptions helped me recognize the limitations and negative effects of perfectionism, paving the way for healthier and more productive approaches to achieving my personal and professional goals.

I am sure when you start to be free from misconceptions of perfectionism, you will get on a fast track of progress in your life.

Put the Heavy Bag of the Past Down and Rise from Your Ashes Like a Phoenix

I've always been fascinated by the phoenix ever since I learned about its incredible healing powers and its ability to rise from its own ashes. The more I read about this mythical bird, the more its story captivated me.

The origins of the phoenix trace back to ancient Egypt, where it was revered as a magnificent bird associated with the worship of the sun god. This bird was as large as an eagle, with brilliant scarlet and golden wings. Only one phoenix lived at a time, and it could live up to 500 years. When the old phoenix sensed its end approaching, it would fly to the city of the Sun God—Heliopolis, Egypt—where it would build a nest atop the Sun Temple, using miraculous herbs and spices.

The sun would then ignite the nest, consuming the old phoenix in flames. From the ashes, a new and young phoenix would rise, flying back to Arabia to begin a new life cycle.

The Greek historian Herodotus is credited with introducing the legend of the magical phoenix to the Western world. After his visit to Egypt and Heliopolis, he shared the story of this incredible bird with the Greek people. In his famous *histories* (fifth century BCE), Herodotus describes various fantastic beasts, including the crocodile, hippopotamus, and phoenix. He recounts how the temple priests spoke of the phoenix: "They have another sacred bird called the phoenix, which I have never seen, except in pictures. Indeed, it is a great rarity, even in Egypt. They tell a story of what this bird does, which does not seem to me to be credible."

Over the centuries, the legend of the phoenix—symbolizing hope and eternity—inspired many, including the Romans, who chose the phoenix as a symbol of their eternal legacy. Roman coins even depicted the head of the emperor on one side and a phoenix on the other.

The phoenix is a bird of eternal hope and healing.

I know you have experienced failures. I know you have endured pain. I understand how your goals and desires may have taken a toll on you. I know how it feels to be aware of your hidden potential, yet struggle to express it to the world. I know you have incomplete goals, like I do, and that the desire to complete them is intense—but even more intense is the pain of seeing them remain unfinished.

That pain is real, but so is hope. Remember, gold must be beaten into sheets and endure high temperatures before it can become a beautiful ornament. Diamonds aren't formed in a day; they are created under immense pressure and heat over years, deep within the darkest layers of coal.

Even the bamboo tree takes three years before it rises above the earth as a green shoot, eventually growing into a towering tree.

Let's rise from our ashes, like the phoenix, and embrace the hope of a new beginning.

Striving for Perfection May Be Stopping You—Embrace Shoshin

As described in various interviews and articles, 23-time Olympic Gold Medalist *Michael Phelps*, arguably the greatest Olympian ever, struggled with a perfectionist mindset. He was obsessed with perfection, and anything less than perfect was unacceptable to him. This obsession later led to greater mental health issues as depression and anxiety. Phelps quickly recognized the problem of perfectionism and learned to focus on the process and progress instead. Working with his therapist, he overcame these challenges and spoke openly about his struggles.

This helped him embrace his imperfections and prioritize well-being over perfectionism.

Similarly, tennis star *Serena Williams* struggled with the idea that anything less than perfect was a failure. She learned to channel her perfectionist tendencies into a drive for self-improvement. Serena focused on self-compassion, recognizing that mistakes are part of the journey and that resilience is the key to success.

Emma Watson, known for her role as Hermione Granger in the "Harry Potter" series, has also spoken about her struggles with perfectionism and imposter syndrome. She felt immense pressure to live up to expectations and was often her harshest critic. Watson realized she needed to improve this part of her thinking. By focusing on self-acceptance and self-care, she overcame the pressure and burden of being perfect all the time.

Mistakes are an essential part of any creative process, and a willingness to experiment, tweak, and twist is required to create something new and novel. Once mistakes and experimentation are integral to any success story, it immediately lifts a heavy burden off our shoulders.

Remember when we were children? We approached each task, each skill, with an eagerness to learn, without prejudice about the teacher or the fellow learners. We enjoyed learning to draw, playing football, riding a bike, and swimming. Though we weren't excellent at first, we kept learning with joy and eagerness, never comparing ourselves to others.

So, what happens as we grow up? What happens when we want to switch careers, start our own business, work in a new country, or start solo traveling? Why do we find it so hard to approach these new challenges with the same beginner's mindset and patience, knowing we'll improve with time? Over the years, we develop preconceived notions and rigid belief systems that create resistance to learning new things and believing it's possible. We become perfectionists rather than learners, making it harder to grow and progress.

Here are some thought patterns of a perfectionist mind that can stop us from growing:

- "I will publish my first book once I have mastered the art of writing," but we never know when we will become masters.

- "I will start traveling solo once I have a decent job," but we may never know when that job will come.

- "I will start rising early in the morning once I have lost weight."

- "I will be happier when I get my dream job."

- "I don't have a friend who plays tennis like me, otherwise I would play daily."

- "I will give 100% effort in my job once I get my dream job."

It's easy to relate to these thought patterns—some of them were my constant companions until recently. But better late than never, I realized that these perfectionist thoughts were my first hurdles on the path to progress.

Let me introduce you to the Japanese concept of **Shoshin**. Shunryu Suzuki talks about Shoshin, which is a concept from Zen Buddhism meaning "beginner's mind."

"In the beginner's mind there are many possibilities, but in the expert's mind there are few," says Suzuki.

It is an amazing power to approach each task with a beginner's mind; it opens a whole new world of possibilities and you will be amazed at how powerful this technique is. Stop thinking like an expert. Start approaching each task with a beginner's mind.

Once we become experienced in any skill, we often close off the learning faculties of our mind, limiting ourselves to new possibilities. It's natural to become rigid once we attain a certain level of expertise—it gives us authority, demonstrates our confidence, and shows others we are in command. But it also makes it easy to fall into the trap of stagnation, like stagnant water in a pond.

Why not be like the flowing waters of a river—always fresh, pristine, powerful, divine, and living?

The Zen Buddhism concept of Shoshin encourages us to understand that we are often the biggest hurdle in our growth. We should approach each day like a beginner—always curious, always happy to learn, and always filled with enthusiasm that today we will learn something new and grow. We must embrace tasks with childlike curiosity, as this is a great secret to leading a life of progress and eternal growth. Practicing Shoshin will protect you from the unnecessary burden of expectations and the stress of becoming an expert.

By embracing Shoshin, you take one step closer to greatness, following the *eternal path of progress in Zen Buddhism.*

Recognizing the Pit of Procrastination as Your Nemesis

Since 2018, I have had an intense desire to write the book you're now holding in your hands. It was painful to see myself struggling daily with the task. I was working as a manager at an oil company, a demanding job that required 10-12 hours of my day. I knew that if I prioritized writing this book, which I wanted so badly, I could create something impactful for the lives of my readers. Yet, I was stuck, unable to complete it, as the years passed by.

My mind constantly made it more difficult, reminding me I had already taken seven years and was still struggling. The thought of abandoning the book to focus on my job, which provided for my family, was tempting. Safety and security of a good, consistent salary always kept me away from striving for my full potential. Despite all the knowledge and wisdom I had gained from books, I wasn't moving forward in life. It was frustrating and painful to see my dreams of publishing my book slipping away.

In March 2014, I faced another life-changing challenge. Until then, I was living in Jaipur with my wife and our 6-month-old daughter. But that March, my deepest fear came alive—I was transferred to a village in the Thar Desert, far west in Rajasthan. The village lacked medical facilities, so I had to move alone, leaving my family behind. It was emotionally devastating.

One day, I decided I couldn't continue in this way. I asked myself what I could do to improve my situation. I decided to objectively assess my progress, habits, and behaviours. My number one hurdle was my ego.

A) Ego: My Greatest Hurdle

Over the years, I had worked hard on many tough challenges, pushing myself to achieve success. God blessed me with many achievements, such as getting into IIT, playing tennis at the national level, and later, gaining admission to IIM. These successes, however, turned my once-humble self into someone arrogant and stubborn, unaware that the poison of ego was slowly dragging me down.

I stopped learning new things and developed an *entitlement mindset*. I began to think I deserved better treatment, which ultimately stunted my growth.

B) Substance Abuse: Falling into the Pit

The freedom that came with leaving home for IIT allowed me to make my own choices, but I fell into bad habits, particularly substance abuse. It started as casual fun but soon became a destructive habit that lasted five years, affecting my health, career, and relationships. However, I eventually realized the damage I was doing to myself and pulled myself out of that pit.

C) Losing My Superpower: Belief in Myself

The most significant loss I faced was losing belief in myself. This realization hit me hardest when I began writing this book. The superpower of believing in my efforts had been the key to all my past successes, yet I had stopped using it. This awareness empowered me to start cultivating self-belief again, along with faith in my ideals, Lord Ram, Lord Hanuman, and Goddess Saraswati.

As we move along our journey of progress, it's crucial to identify areas of improvement and consciously work on them. If we want to improve our present condition and aim to become world class, we must understand the root cause of our problems.

Procrastination: The Monster That Hinders Progress

As we journey towards progress, it's essential to identify areas for improvement and consciously work on them.

Understanding the root cause of our challenges is crucial if we aim to elevate our current condition and achieve world-class results.

Let's examine this monster called procrastination, which stands as the biggest hurdle in our path to progress.

Procrastination is the act of delaying or postponing tasks or decisions, often leading to stress, anxiety, or negative outcomes. It involves choosing more pleasurable or less demanding activities over tasks that require immediate attention, even though we know that this delay may have adverse consequences.

How to Recognize Procrastination:

We Delay by choice: Procrastination is a choice, not imposed by external factors, but by our own decision to delay necessary actions. For example, when I was working on publishing my first book, I often postponed actions, thinking there was enough time. In reality, I was afraid of facing the challenges of learning new skills. In fact, I was afraid to give my hundred percent, as I was fearful of meeting failure again.

We avoid tasks: We often avoid tasks that seem difficult, unpleasant, or overwhelming. I avoided editing my book for two whole years because my ego couldn't accept that I lacked the editing skills, so I never started learning the new skill of editing and struggled for years stuck with limited skill of editing.

We go for Immediate Gratification: We procrastinate in favour of activities that offer immediate pleasure or are less demanding. I delayed completing my book by opting for instant gratifications, like eating out, watching Netflix, or scrolling through Instagram for hours.

We do not care about negative future consequences. Despite knowing that procrastination leads to stress, guilt, missed deadlines, or decreased performance, we continue to procrastinate. I knew that not finishing my book was creating a stressful future for myself, yet I kept falling into old habits, avoiding the path of progress.

We hide our emotional weakness: Procrastination is often a way to manage negative emotions related to a task, such as fear of failure, anxiety, or self-doubt. When I set the goal of publishing a book in 2018, it was an ambitious aim that I knew would fulfil me and restore my confidence. Yet, the path from imagination to expression required consistent action, which I struggled to take because of fears rooted in past failures and the fear of being judged.

Examples of Procrastination:

Academic Procrastination: A student waits until the last minute to start studying for exams, despite knowing the importance of adequate preparation.

Workplace Procrastination: An employee delays starting a major project and instead focuses on trivial tasks, risking the project deadline.

Everyday Procrastination: Putting off mundane tasks like doing laundry or paying bills until they become urgent.

Why We Procrastinate:

There are many reasons we procrastinate. The root lies within our limiting beliefs, which are very hard to recognise and even if we can recognise them, it takes consistent effort to complete remove them.

Fear of failure: Fear of not succeeding or meeting high standards can lead to avoidance. This was my biggest hurdle. The fear of failure often paralyzed me, preventing me from taking the steps towards progress. Thoughts like,

"I'm not a world-class writer yet; who will read my book?" haunted me and became my greatest obstacle.

Perfectionism: The desire to achieve perfection can cause delaying tasks until we feel conditions are perfect. I often compared my work to past accolades, avoiding the present realities. I would reread my first draft, become overly critical, and compare my writing to world-class authors like Robin Sharma. And eventually delay my work endlessly.

Lack of motivation: When tasks aren't inherently rewarding or interesting, it's challenging to muster the motivation to start. I love reading books and could spend hours expanding my knowledge. But for writing, sometimes words flowed like water from a Himalayan spring, while at other times, expressing my thoughts felt like a Herculean task.

Indecisiveness: Difficulty in deciding can lead to postponing tasks that require commitment. When confidence is lost, we become dependent on external circumstances and the choices of others. We let ourselves be carried by the flow, becoming indecisive and allowing others to decide for us.

Overwhelm: Feeling overwhelmed by the scope or complexity of a task can lead to avoidance. Projects with tight deadlines or high stakes, like completing a research paper in two months or preparing a client presentation worth millions, can create feelings of overwhelm, leading to procrastination.

The Story of Beethoven: The Unfinished Symphony

Ludwig van Beethoven was born in Bonn, Germany, in 1770. His father, Johann van Beethoven, a musician himself, recognized his son's prodigious talent and pushed him, often harshly, to become a talented musician. Despite this challenging relationship, Beethoven showed remarkable progress and began performing publicly by age seven, composing original music by twelve.

In 1792, Beethoven moved to Vienna, where he studied under the famed composer Joseph Haydn. He quickly established himself as a well-known pianist and composer, gaining patronage from Vienna's aristocracy.

However, around 1796, Beethoven began experiencing hearing loss, which worsened. By 1801, he described the "buzzing" and "ringing" in his ears in letters to friends, a devastating condition for a musician. Despite seeking various treatments, his hearing continued to deteriorate, and by 1814, he was almost completely deaf.

This hearing loss profoundly affected his social life and mental health. In 1802, he wrote the famous *Heiligenstadt Testament*, a letter to his brothers expressing his deep grief and pain, lamenting that he could no longer enjoy music or public life.

The period from 1803 to 1812 marked his peak creativity, but his hearing loss fueled his obsession with perfectionism, leading to self-doubt and procrastination. In 1814, he began his famous Symphony No. 10, which was never completed; only sketches and fragments remain.

Yet Beethoven's genius shone through. After struggling with his hearing loss for nearly 18 years, he accepted his condition and found innovative ways to "hear" his music. He would press his ear hard against the piano to feel the vibrations and relied on his deep understanding of music theory and vivid imagination to compose. This period saw the creation of some of his most extraordinary works, including the Ninth Symphony (1824), featuring the famous "Ode to Joy."

Beethoven passed away on March 26, 1827, in Vienna. Despite his struggles with perfectionism, procrastination, and deafness, he left a legacy of music that continues to inspire the world. His life is a testament to the power of resilience, creativity, and the acceptance of imperfection.

Important points from first chapter:

- Most of the times your solution lies in the challenges you are facing. You just need to change your perspective about the challenge.
- It is possible to convert your greatest weakness into your greatest strength.
- Perfectionism is a hurdle on your path of progress. Choose progress over perfection.
- Do not let your past rule over your present. Be free in the present to create a future of abundance and freedom.
- It is always possible to start a fresh even if you are feeling completely defeated, broken, ruined and lost forever. Be inspired by the story of the mysterious bird Phoenix, which always rises from its ashes.
- Practice Shoshin (Beginner's mind): To start all tasks with a beginner's mind. Always curious, happy to learn, always enthusiastic, free from the past, joyfully present, always open to all possibilities, to lead a life of progress and eternal growth. Shoshin protects us from the burden of experience and stress of being an expert.
- Recognise the pit of procrastination: Fear of failure, going for perfection, lack of motivation and indecisiveness leads you to procrastination.

In the next chapter, we will deep dive into " why you cannot complete your goals " and check Are You Tied to a Small Rope Like the Elephant?

Jot down your thoughts after reading the first chapter.

Reflect on the new insights you have gained and try to apply them to your life situation.

Chapter 2- Why are you not able to complete your most desirable goal

"Dig into the roots instead of just hacking at the leaves." — Anthony J. D'Angelo

Once upon a time, a young man in India left his home in search of truth. He longed to understand the deeper meaning of life so that he could follow the true path and become a successful person.

He wandered through jungles for days, surviving on whatever food and water he could find. Eventually, he settled into a solitary life in a hut near a river in the Himalayas. Every morning, after bathing in the icy river, he meditated. He did this faithfully for five years. Over time, he became healthier and more peaceful, but he knew deep down that he was still far from the truth he sought.

Realizing he needed guidance, he sought a wise person. He traveled south, towards the state of Madhya Pradesh. There, by the bank of a river, under the shade of a banyan tree, he met a sage meditating.

"I have been meditating in the northern Himalayas for five years in search of truth," the young man says. "But I know I am not progressing. Can you guide me?"

"Yes," replies the sage. "Continue your journey south, towards the state of Karnataka. There, among the elephants, you will find the truth."

The young man followed the sage's advice and continued his journey south. For over three months, he travelled through dense jungles, evading wild animals and surviving on fruits and berries. Finally, he arrived in Karnataka, the land of elephants. He was overjoyed, thinking he was finally close to discovering the ultimate truth that would lead him to glory.

The next morning, he went to a nearby river to bathe. There, he saw the king's elephants, majestic creatures being trained for war. As he observed them, he noticed something surprising: these massive elephants were tied to small ropes, with the ropes secured to wooden stakes in the ground.

Puzzled, the young man asks the mahout, "How is it that such strong, powerful elephants are held by such small ropes?"

The mahout replies, "These elephants have been conditioned to be tied to these ropes since birth. They've become so accustomed to it they believe they are bound and cannot break free."

"But if the elephant gave a powerful tug, it could easily break free," the young man observed.

"Yes," the mahout agrees, "that is the truth."

At that moment, the young man found the answer he had been searching for. He realized that, like the elephants, he too had been bound by invisible ropes—his limiting beliefs. Filled with newfound clarity, he returned home eager to live life with a renewed zest, free of all bondages. He had discovered that he was always free.

The origin of this story can be traced back to Indian scriptures, but the moral remains as fresh and relevant today as it was 5,000 years ago when people left their homes to become sannyasins in search of truth.

We are born free and remain free until we tie ourselves to the invisible ropes of limiting beliefs, such as "I am not strong enough," "I don't have enough money," "I'm not smart enough," "I can't manage a team," "I can't start a business," or "I'm not courageous enough." These self-imposed limitations hold us back from realizing our true potential.

The best part is we can set ourselves free again by breaking the ropes easily. Are you ready to break free?

Apply This Truth to Your Life

Consider whether you, too, are like the strong elephant tied to a small rope—stuck in limiting beliefs and habitual thinking patterns. Below, I've listed some of my limiting beliefs I overcame once I recognized them:

Thinking Like an Elephant Tied to a Small Rope

- I need other people to be happy.

- I don't have enough money to start a business aligned with my passion.

- I love tennis, but I can't enjoy it now because I don't have other talented players to play with.

- Having too much money is not good for me.

- My parents didn't support me when I needed them most; otherwise, I could have been world class.

- My wife is not aligned with my goals; otherwise, I could achieve success at a faster pace.

Thinking Like a Free Man (with no Rope)

- I am always happy, no matter the situation.

- I will start with whatever resources I have. Money is a byproduct of excellent skills applied to serve the maximum number of people.

- I love playing tennis, and I will continue to play and improve throughout my life.

- I will have an abundance of health, wealth, and wisdom in life.

- My parents did their best to educate me. Now it's my turn to do my best to raise my family and serve the world by applying my management and writing skills.

- My wife and I have unique talents. We respect each other's freedom to live joyfully and support each other in living a life of freedom.

Can you see the difference in thinking? This happens when you realize you are always free. A single thought holds the potential to free you for life.

Transforming Limiting Beliefs about Powerful Thoughts of Freedom

1. **Identify Your Limiting Beliefs:**

   - Take a moment to reflect on the thoughts and beliefs that are holding you back. Write each one down on paper.

2. **Create Empowering Counter-Beliefs:**

   - Next to each limiting belief, write a corresponding belief that embodies freedom and possibility. This new belief should be the opposite of the limiting one.

3. **Commit to Your New Beliefs:**

   o On a separate sheet of paper, list your new empowering beliefs. This will serve as your personal manifesto of freedom.

4. **Ingrain Your New Beliefs:**

   o Every night before you sleep, and every morning when you wake up, read and write these empowering thoughts. Do this with a genuine sense of joy and excitement, knowing that you are stepping into a life of freedom, truth, and happiness.

5. **Embrace Positive Emotions:**

   o As you practice this exercise, cultivate feelings of joy and happiness, especially before sleeping and upon waking. These emotions will reinforce your new beliefs.

6. **Commit to 30 Days:**

   o Consistency is key. Commit to doing this exercise for the next 30 days, allowing your new beliefs to take root in your subconscious.

7. **Observe the Changes:**

   o Pay attention to the shifts in your thoughts, emotions, and overall life experience. Notice how these new beliefs are positively affecting your life.

8. **Maintain the Practice:**

   o If you find this exercise beneficial, continue practicing it beyond the 30 days. Make it a part of your daily routine to sustain your newfound freedom and growth.

Do You Have the Right Skills and Knowledge for Your Goals?

In his famous book *Flow*, author Mihaly Csikszentmihalyi emphasizes the importance of having the right skill set to achieve a state of flow—a continuous feeling of happiness and fulfilment while pursuing a goal. To reach this state, it's crucial to evaluate whether your skills align with the goals you've set.

For instance, as the university tennis captain, I represented my university in a national-level men's tennis tournament in 2013. Now, I have made a goal to play at Wimbledon by 2026. But can you see the mismatch between this goal and my current skill set? Without turning professional or developing the skills required to compete at Wimbledon, I've set a goal that is far beyond my current capabilities.

A more appropriate goal, aligned with my current skills, would be to hire a coach and turn professional in tennis by 2026.

Based on this knowledge, you must match your skills with your current goals. This will keep you on track with progress and happiness. You will find your flow zone.

Align Your Goals with Your Skill Levels

It's important to assess whether your goals match your current skill levels. This alignment helps ensure your goals are challenging yet achievable, allowing you to grow without feeling overwhelmed.

- If Your Goal Exceeds Your Skill Set: If you realize your current goal is too high for your current skills, consider adjusting your goal to match where you are right now. This doesn't mean abandoning your bigger dream, but setting a more realistic, immediate goal that serves as a stepping stone. For instance, instead of aiming directly for Wimbledon, I should focus on improving my ranking and gaining more experience in competitive tennis.

- If Your Goal Is Below Your Skill Set: if you find your goal is too easy based on your abilities, it's time to raise your expectations. Pushing your goals higher will challenge you to reach your full potential. For example, if I am already a strong tennis player, I should set my sights on tougher competitions or aim for a higher performance level.

Regularly aligning your goals with your current skills ensures that you're always moving forward at a pace that fosters growth while keeping your ambitions realistic. This approach keeps you motivated and focused on continuous improvement.

Check if Your Ego is Your Friend or Enemy

Thinking *"I am outstanding"* can be powerful—it keeps you motivated, pushing you to do your best and achieve significant results. But thinking *"I am perfect, and others are beneath me"* is a limiting belief. It will hinder your progress.

A better way to think is: *"I am the best, and I'm becoming better and better in my profession because*

I practice daily, and I'm committed to excellence."
This thought of a friendly ego.

However, if you think: *"I'm the best and better than others because I was the best in the past and have already achieved a lot,"* that's enemy ego at work—a belief that will hold you back.

Your ego should always push you to put in more effort, commit to daily growth, and strive for improvement. It shouldn't allow you to become complacent and rest on your past successes. This way, *your ego becomes a friend, driving your progress.*

I was caught in the trap of enemy ego for almost seven years, from 2013 to 2020. After completing my education from prestigious institutions like IIT and IIM, my ego made me believe I had done everything to deserve success, and I could now rest on my past achievements.

It took me seven years to realize that my enemy ego was one of the biggest roadblocks in my journey of growth. But as the saying goes, *better late than never.* I started reading books that opened my mind to the fact that there was still so much more to learn and experience in life. Once I embraced this wisdom, I consciously began to apply it.

For example, while working as a Manager of M&C in the oil industry, I often found myself emotionally entangled in petty issues, trying to prove to others that I was more knowledgeable or superior. This behaviour drained me emotionally and wasted my time and energy on non-productive things.

Once I recognized my ego was trapping me in these small, insignificant issues, I consciously worked on it. After 2-3 years of practice, I detached myself from such distractions. This saved me a significant amount of time and energy, which I could then channel into completing the very book you're reading now.

See If You Need a Mentor or a Guru

For those of us who seek a life of freedom, abundance, and purpose—one filled with passion, love, gratitude, and wisdom—a life where you are the creator of your future, where you can travel and embrace adventure without seeking approval from bosses, the key is a lifelong commitment to learning.

We can't afford to sit back and say, "I'm 35, earning well, enjoying a good social status, so there's nothing more I need to learn."

The moment you think that way, you're done—stagnant and finished. You become like a still pool, slowly stinking with limited knowledge and a *growing enemy ego*.

All those who have achieved greatness in any field have one thing in common—they *continuously seek mentors* and gurus to guide them along the way.

Before becoming world famous for her novel, *I Know Why the Caged Bird Sings,* Maya Angelou had to find her path, just like all of us.

In the 1950s, as she struggled to establish herself as a writer, she moved to New York and joined Harlem's Writer's Guild. It was here that she met James Baldwin, an established and respected writer known for his work on race and identity in America.

Baldwin quickly recognized Angelou's immense talent. She had a powerful story, but she was hesitant and fearful about expressing it with full confidence. She was afraid that sharing her story through writing would make her vulnerable and expose her deepest emotions.

Having faced his challenges as a writer, Baldwin understood what she was going through. He acted more like a friend than a mentor; he encouraged Angelou to embrace her story and express her fears openly. He showed her the *power of authenticity* that every brilliant writer can tap into.

Baldwin was not only a master of the craft, but he also knew the nuances and tools required to transform an average writer into a master. The turning point in Angelou's journey came when Baldwin introduced her to the editor, Robert Loomis. Loomis saw the potential in her story and urged her to write her autobiography, but she was still reluctant, held back by her fear of vulnerability.

At this critical moment, Baldwin shared another key insight—he told her that her story had the *power to affect lives* and bring meaningful change to people going through similar struggles. That her words could inspire and help others finally outweighed her fear of being vulnerable.

With this newfound purpose, Maya Angelou began writing her autobiography, and the rest is history. She wrote the world-famous book *I Know Why the Caged Bird Sings,* a masterpiece that continues to inspire readers around the world.

Finding the right mentor is crucial on the journey of growth. Baldwin introduced her to the tools of mastering the craft as a friend—providing emotional support, inspiring her, and helping her believe in herself. He showed her that her story had the potential to change millions of lives.

Greatness is often sparked in the company of great people. So, if you feel stuck or unable to move forward on your path, look around. There are people in your field who have already achieved success, who are kind-hearted, and who are ready to share their experiences. These people are often willing to mentor you on your journey to progress and greatness.

So if you are finding it challenging to progress in your journey, it is always advisable to seek for a mentorship.

Find Your WHY, Write It Every Day, and Read It Before Sleeping

Chasing your goals without knowing your "why" is like a tiger trying to fish like a shark in the ocean, an elephant trying to run as fast as a cheetah, or a fish attempting to climb a tree. The importance of knowing your purpose in life cannot be overstated.

Albert Einstein understood this well: *"Everybody is a genius. But if you judge a fish by its ability to climb a tree, it will live its whole life believing that it is stupid."*

A powerful example of finding one's purpose comes from Viktor Frankl, whose story stands as a testament to resilience and meaning even in the most devastating circumstances.

In 1942, Frankl's life was torn apart when he and his family were sent to concentration camps. His parents, brother, and pregnant wife all perished. Frankl himself endured horrific conditions at Auschwitz, facing starvation, forced labour, disease, and constant fear of death. Amid this unimaginable suffering, Frankl observed human behaviour, noticing that some prisoners could maintain their inner strength and survive, while others, who lost hope, soon perished.

This observation became the foundation of his life's work, which he later called "*Logotherapy*"—a method of finding purpose and living meaningfully. Frankl concluded that those who held onto a vision of a hopeful future or a *sense of purpose* were far more likely to survive than those who had no vision or hope.

Frankl later documented this profound insight in his book *Man's Search for Meaning*, published in 1946. This small but impactful book has inspired millions, and I find it a must-read for anyone seeking to overcome adversity. If you haven't read it, I highly recommend it.

Frankl found meaning in the worst of circumstances. He kept visualizing the day he would reunite with his wife, never losing hope despite the terror surrounding him. His story is a powerful testament to the human *capacity to choose how we react* to even the most difficult situations.

No matter where you are or what you're going through, you have the power to choose your response and move closer to finding your "why." Frankl teaches us that when people understand their "why," they can endure almost any "how."

Here are some questions that will help you find your own "why":

Question 1: *What are my core values, and how do they influence my decisions?*

Example: *When have I felt most proud of myself, and what values was I honoring in those moments?*

Take your own time while answering these questions. You might take a day or two. These are life-changing questions and will help you give direction for the rest of your life. So don't be in a hurry, just let the questions sink in. The correct answers will flow.

For me it was getting an education from the best Indian Institutes IIT and IIM, always filled me with pride and fulfilment. I honor my commitment to excellence, honesty, consistent hard work, and resilience with these moments.

Similarly, you try to find the answer for you.

Question 2: *What are the moments in my life when I felt most alive, energized, and fulfilled?*

Example: *What was I doing, who was I with, and what impact was I having during those moments?* This will help you understand your genuine passions and inner drive.

For me, it is playing tennis and striving to learn and improve my tennis skills fills me with energy and fulfilment.

Similarly, you try to find the answer for you.

Question 3: *What recurring themes and patterns do I notice in the feedback I receive from others?* Reflection Example: *What do people often thank me for,* *and what do they seek my help with?* Often, others can clearly see our strengths and passions, even when we can't.

For me, it is my sporting abilities and passion for excellence that people often come to thank me and seek my help with.

Similarly, you try to find the answer for you.

Question 4: *"If I knew I could not fail, what would I be doing with my life?"*

"What goals and dreams do I keep coming back to, even if they seem unrealistic?"

The fear of failure often clouds our desires and prevents us from taking action to pursue our passions.

For me it will write books and affecting lives of as many people as I could and seek freedom and abundance with my writing. Also, I will continue to play tennis throughout my life and keep improving my tennis skills with age.

Similarly, you try to find the answer for you.

Question 5: *"How do I want to be remembered?"* *"What legacy do I want to leave behind?"*

"What stories do I want people to tell about me after I'm gone? What contributions will I have made to the world?"

Answering these questions forces us to think long-term. They introduce a vital insight: the idea of mortality brings clarity of purpose and helps us live more authentically.

This is a significant question and will surely force you to think clearly towards your why. I love this question.

These questions are not so easy to answer, but yes, if you give them enough time, the answers will flow from your heart and you will know more about yourself.

For me: I want to leave a legacy where I affected lives of people through the skill of reading books and showing them a path of clarity and wisdom. I want my legacy where I make it possible for a common to think that abundance in all areas is possible with consistent work by following a proven track.

Important points from second chapter:

- Check Are You Tied to a Small Rope Like the Elephant?
- Break away your ropes of limiting beliefs and start to think freely. Transform your limiting beliefs into powerful thoughts of freedom.
- Match your skills with your goals for enjoying the flow of living.
- Check whether your ego is your friend or your enemy.

- Check if you need a mentor on your journey. Role of a suitable mentor is crucial on the path of progress.
- Find your "why", write it down, practice reading it every day before you sleep. Your "why" is your North start, which gives purpose and direction to life.

Jot down your thoughts after reading the second chapter:

Reflect on the new insights you have gained and apply them to your life situation.

Chapter 3- Scientific Insights for Progress

"The great thing about science is that it provides tools and methods to solve problems we didn't even know we had." — Carl Sagan

The Power of Small Wins: The Progress Principle

A recent study by Teresa Amabile and Steven Kramer at Harvard Business School offers simple yet powerful insights into how we can make consistent progress in daily life:

A) Daily Progress Boosts Motivation
One key finding suggests that making small, consistent progress provides an incredible boost to motivation. This sense of achievement creates a snowball effect, improving emotional well-being and increasing engagement in work. We've all experienced it — when we accomplish even a minor task, it motivates us to tackle the next one. When that's successful too, we feel empowered, and this momentum helps us achieve bigger goals.

B) Small Wins Accumulate

Think of the story of the thirsty crow, who repeatedly drops pebbles into a pot until the water rises high enough for him to drink. In much the same way, small wins accumulate over time and lead to significant success. Just like compound interest in mathematics, these minor victories build on one another, bringing substantial rewards in the long run.

C) Positive Feedback Loop

Achieving even minor success creates a positive feedback loop. The sense of accomplishment boosts confidence, leading to increased motivation and further progress. This cycle helps sustain ongoing growth and achievement.

D) Focus on Incremental Steps

Research shows that breaking larger goals into small, manageable tasks, customized to your specific situation, makes those goals more achievable. This approach reduces feelings of overwhelm and helps combat procrastination, making the journey toward your objectives more manageable.

E) Impact on Workplace Performance

The study also found that employees who felt a sense of progress in their daily tasks were more productive, creative, and satisfied with their jobs.

Focusing on daily small wins is the key to long-term success.

Psychologist and Stanford professor Carol Dweck spent over a decade researching the concept of Growth Mindset. Through her work, she observed children in educational settings, presenting them with intractable problems and tracking their reactions and performance.

Her research revealed two distinct responses: some children thrived on the challenge, viewing it as an opportunity to learn, while others became discouraged and gave up easily. This discovery led to the identification of two types of mindsets:

- Growth Mindset: The belief that abilities and intelligence can be developed through consistent effort, learning, and perseverance.

- Fixed Mindset: The belief that abilities and intelligence are static and cannot be changed.

From these observations, several important insights emerged:

A) Belief in Growth and Development:

A person with a growth mindset believes that skills and intelligence can be improved with dedication and hard work. Such individuals embrace challenges, viewing failure as an opportunity to learn rather than a setback. People with a growth mindset develop a love for the learning process, are resilient, and willingly embrace obstacles—traits essential for long-term success.

B) Practical Impact of Growth Mindset:

Dweck's findings conclude that a growth mindset—the belief in one's ability to improve through effort—leads to remarkable results in practical environments like schools, universities, and workplaces. The potential for growth through persistence becomes a powerful motivator.

C) Empowerment Through Belief:

Perhaps the most valuable insight from Carol's research is the power of belief. Believing in your ability to grow and change can be transformative. People who apply this mindset in their lives have achieved extraordinary success in their fields.

Examples of Growth Mindset in Action

Michael Jordan–Basketball Legend

Jordan famously says, "I have missed over 9,000 shots in my career. I have lost almost 300 games. 26 times, I've been trusted to take the game-winning shot and missed. I've failed over and repeated in my life. And that is why I succeed."
His relentless commitment to growth, despite failures, is a perfect embodiment of the growth mindset.

J. K. Rowling–Author of the Harry Potter Series Before her manuscript was accepted, Rowling faced multiple rejections and endured financial and personal hardships. Her growth mindset allowed her to embrace challenges, keep going without quitting, and remain resilient on her path to glory. Her perseverance turned her into one of the most famous authors in the world.

Oprah Winfrey–Media Mogul

Oprah's journey from poverty and abuse to becoming a media icon exemplifies the growth mindset. She consistently believed in her ability to improve, grow, and make a difference, using her challenges as stepping stones to success.

Elon Musk–Entrepreneur and Innovator Musk, CEO of Tesla and SpaceX, encountered many setbacks, including near bankruptcy, in both companies. Without formal education in engineering or aerospace, he taught himself by reading books and applying that knowledge practically. His belief in learning any skill if one is willing and committed to growth reflects the essence of the growth mindset.

Serena Williams–Tennis Champion In 2017, Serena was 8 weeks pregnant when she won the Australian Open. After giving birth, she faced severe health complications, including life-threatening blood clots. Despite pundits doubting her return, Serena, driven by her belief in growth, worked on her tennis and physical strength while raising her daughter, Olympia. Within two years, she reached the finals of four Grand Slam, showing the world the power of perseverance and the growth mindset.

Steve Jobs–Return to Apple in 1997 In 1985, Steve Jobs was ousted from the company he co-founded after a major disagreement with the board. It was not only humiliating but soul-crushing. Despite this, Jobs refused to give up. He founded NeXT, a computer platform company, and led Pixar to create Toy Story, the first fully computer-animated feature film. In 1996, Apple gained NeXT, and Jobs returned to the company, which was on the verge of bankruptcy. Instead

of being overwhelmed by its financial crisis, Jobs saw the challenge as an opportunity. He streamlined Apple's product line and introduced innovations like the iMac, iPod, iPhone, and iPad—revolutionizing the tech industry. His story illustrates how believing in growth, resilience, and continuous improvement helped him rise again and change the world.

The Role of Grit: Perseverance and Passion

Angela Duckworth, a former math teacher in New York City, noticed something intriguing: her most successful students weren't necessarily the most talented or intelligent, but the most determined. This observation led her to groundbreaking research on grit, beginning at the US Military Academy at West Point.

One of the most inspiring stories from her research involves a cadet named Sarah. Sarah wasn't the strongest, fastest, or smartest in her class, but she had an unshakable will. At West Point, students must first pass a rigorous selection process and then survive "Beast Barracks," a seven-week program designed to push them to their physical and mental limits. Many cadets, unable to cope with the extreme pressure, dropped out.

Sarah struggled more than most. The physical demands were intense, and she wasn't a natural athlete. But despite the difficulty, Sarah was determined not to quit. Each day, she pushed her limits, visualizing how proud she'd feel when she finally completed her training. Her vision kept her going. Eventually, her grit not only helped her finish but also excel in her training, earning her a leadership role among her peers.

Sarah's journey exemplifies Duckworth's key finding: grit—passion and perseverance—often plays a larger role in success than talent or intelligence.

Key Findings from Duckworth's Research:

1. **Gritty people are passionate about their work**: Duckworth notes that "Passion begins with intrinsically enjoying what you do."

2. **They practice**: Without discipline and effort, even the most talented people won't reach their full potential.

3. **They have purpose**: Passion matures when people believe their work has meaning.

4. **They are hopeful**: "Hope defines every stage of grit," Duckworth writes. It is this "rising-to-the-occasion" perseverance that sustains gritty people through challenges.

The best part? Grit isn't something you either have or don't—it's a trait you can cultivate. "You can grow your grit from the inside out," Duckworth writes.

Grit isn't just found in famous success stories; it's also present in everyday life—like the single mother working multiple jobs to provide her children with the best education.

The Grit Scale: How Gritty You Are?

Duckworth developed a simple tool, the Grit Scale, to help individuals assess their perseverance and passion. Try it for yourself:

For each statement below, rate yourself on a scale from 1 to 5:

- **1 = Not at all like me**

- **2 = Not much like me**

- **3 = Somewhat like me**

- **4 = Mostly like me**

- **5 = Very much like me**

1. **Consistency of Interest**

    - New ideas and projects sometimes distract me from previous ones.

    - I have been obsessed with a certain idea or project for a short time but later lost interest.

    - I often set a goal but later choose to pursue a different one.

    - I have difficulty maintaining focus on projects that take longer than a few months to complete.

2. **Perseverance of Effort**

    - I finish whatever I begin.

    - Setbacks don't discourage me; I don't give up easily.

o   I am a hard worker.

o   I am diligent and persistent.

Scoring:

- **Consistency of Interest Score**: Calculate the average of items 1–4 (reverse-scored).

- **Perseverance of Effort Score**: Calculate the average of items 5–8.

- **Overall Grit Score**: Average all eight items.

Interpreting Your Score:

- **High Grit Score (Closer to 5)**: You're likely persistent and consistent in pursuing long-term goals.

- **Low Grit Score (Closer to 1)**: You may struggle with sticking to long-term goals and persisting through challenges.

Building Your Grit:

1. **Daily Persistence**: Choose a challenging task you're passionate about and commit to doing it every day for the next 30 days, no matter the obstacles.

2. **Visualization**: Practice visualizing the completion of your long-term goal, just as Sarah did at West Point. This mental imagery will help you push through tough times.

3. **Reflection Journal**: Keep a journal where you document your daily challenges and wins. Focus on how you overcame obstacles and continued forward, even when things got tough.

Grit, like any skill, can be cultivated. With practice, persistence, and a clear vision, you can become grittier and achieve your long-term goals.

The science of delayed gratification (Marshmallow Test): A research story

In the late 1960s and early 1970s, a groundbreaking experiment at Stanford University transformed our understanding of self-control and long-term success. This experiment, known as the Marshmallow Test, was led by psychologist Walter Mischel, who was deeply passionate about exploring the concept of delayed gratification.

The Experiment: The Marshmallow Test

In the study, young children, ages 4 to 6, were invited to a room and seated at a table. In front of each child was a single marshmallow. The researchers presented the children with a choice: they could either eat the marshmallow immediately or wait for 15 minutes. If they waited, they would be rewarded with a second marshmallow.

The results of the experiment were astonishing. Mischel followed up with the children over the years and discovered that those who waited for the second marshmallow performed better academically, had stronger social skills, and achieved greater financial success as adults. This simple test highlighted the immense power of self-control and the ability to delay immediate gratification.

The Takeaway

This research teaches us that real, long-term success often requires resisting the allure of quick rewards. By applying the principles of delayed gratification, we learn to embrace the discomfort of the "messy middle"—the period of frustration, failure, and rejection. It is through enduring this stage that we grow and move closer to our goals. Being "incomplete" is part of the process; it's a journey toward a more refined and fulfilled version of ourselves.

Those who master the art of delayed gratification take one significant step closer to progress and success. With small, consistent efforts, we can stay focused on our goals and build a future that is truly rewarding.

Neuroplasticity: Rewiring the brain for progress

In his groundbreaking work on the brain's ability to rewire itself, Dr. Michael Merzenich, a pioneering neuroscientist at the University of California, San Francisco (UCSF), changed our understanding of the brain's capacity to adapt and grow. His research challenged the long-held belief that the brain's structure becomes fixed after early childhood.

The Experiment:

Merzenich and his team conducted experiments on monkeys, surgically altering the nerves in their hands—nerves that would typically signal specific areas in the brain. Contrary to prior beliefs, the brain didn't remain static. Instead, it began reorganizing itself. New neural pathways formed, and the brain areas that previously processed signals from the altered nerves began to receive input from other regions in the hand.

The experiment was later expanded to humans. Targeted exercises were given to individuals with language and learning difficulties, and the results were astonishing. Not only did the participants improve in the specific areas they worked on, but they also showed broader cognitive gains. This proved that the brain's plasticity could be harnessed not just for injury recovery but for various areas of growth.

Unique Insight:

Merzenich's work offered a revolutionary understanding: the brain is not a static organ but a dynamic, ever-changing system.

How Does This Insight Help Us?

This discovery opens up exciting possibilities for personal progress and growth. Neuroplasticity, once seen primarily as a tool for injury recovery, can now transform our lives by developing new ways of thinking and acting. Whether it's mastering a new language, learning to play a musical instrument, or breaking free from limiting habits, the brain's ability to rewire itself means that change is always possible.

Reflect and Apply:

I encourage you to reflect on one area of your life where you feel stuck or limited—an area that could benefit from change.

Let me share one of my own. I had an excellent memory during my childhood and until high school. However, because of some poor habits, including substance abuse, I believe my ability to recall things has diminished compared to my earlier days.

Now, think about an area in your life where you feel held back. Is there something that limits your progress?

Action Steps:

Now that we know the brain is not static but a continuously developing organ, we can work on our limitations and turn them into strengths.

In my case, I've started simple exercises like daily affirmations to improve my memory.

Before going to bed, I say to myself,

"I am always calm and stable. I am always happy, which helps me recall things easily. I have an excellent memory. Thank you, God."

By consistently practicing this affirmation for 30 days, I believe my memory will improve. I'll consciously attempt to remember things that are important to my growth.

Similarly, you can find exercises for your own areas of improvement.

 For instance, if you've gained weight and want to lose it while boosting your self-confidence, you might start with this affirmation:

"I am healthy and confident, and I go to the gym daily."

Pair this with regular gym visits, and over time, with consistent effort, you'll begin to see positive changes.

The Takeaway:

Dr. Michael Merzenich's research not only gives us hope to improve in every area of our lives, but also provides scientific proof that the brain is a dynamic, ever-changing system. This means it's always possible to change our lives for the better.

We just need to find the right exercises for our specific areas of improvement—and when we do, we'll experience a new level of freedom.

- Small daily wins give you much required momentum for consistent progress in life.
- Growth mindset: The belief that abilities and intelligence can be developed through consistent effort, learning, and perseverance. Practice a growth mindset to overcome any challenge by developing new skills and abilities.
- Grit: Perseverance and passion play a much greater role in success as compared to other factors, like intellectual capabilities. It is not the most intelligent, but the most determined who is more likely to succeed in the long run.
- Learn to embrace the "messy middle", a period of frustration, failure and rejection before you taste the sweet success.
- Brain is a dynamic and ever changing system. So it is always possible to rewire our brains, at any stage of life, that will help to progress faster.

Jot down your thoughts after reading the third chapter:

Reflect on the new insights you have gained and apply them to your life situation.

Chapter 4: Revisit Your goals and redefine them

" A Goal is not always meant to be reached; it often serves simply as something to aim at"

Bruce Lee

"We set goals to find freedom, joy, and happiness in life, only to find ourselves stuck, unhappy, and struggling." "Our goals liberate us, not to cage us." — Pushpendra Singh

If you find yourself entangled and struggling with your goals—unable to complete them, and they have become a constant source of disappointment and misery—then we need to change some fundaments in your life situation.

Understand Your Life Stage and Revisit Your Goals

At different stages of life, we may find ourselves in various relationships with our goals. It's important to revisit and refine them based on where we are now.

Consider the example of a professor at an MBA institute. He was once a prolific student, a champion football player, always taking part in team events, full of life. But today, he is married with two daughters—one in 8th grade, the other in 12th. He has no goals and is fearful of making new ones. For him, it's crucial to break free from procrastination and start forming fresh goals that fit his current stage of life.

Now, consider a business executive who has well-defined goals for every aspect of his life—his company, family, and personal goals. However, he feels burnt out and unable to find a way forward. In his case, the problem may focus on too many goals at once. By eliminating some of them, he could streamline his efforts and increase his progress.

Last, let's take the example of a sales agent who is hitting all his sales targets. He has a son excelling in college, a loving wife who is happy with his progress, and yet, he senses something is off. He is anxious and worried all day. For him, it's not about achieving more goals, but about achieving them with more joy and less stress.

There is no one-size-fits-all solution. You need to assess your goals according to your life situation.

The Power of Small Goals

No matter what you're facing, no matter how deep you've fallen into failure, how ashamed or weak you feel, the truth of progress is simple: **get up, start small, and set new goals.** This is the key to moving forward in life.

Imagine a ship in the ocean without a captain—it's destined to sink or crash into something. That's the fate of most people without goals. After completing my MBA from one of India's top institutes, I failed to grasp how important it was to create new goals. I lacked direction and focus and wasted nearly 4–5 years of my life.

But over time, after spending years in self-reflection and reading countless books, I began to understand myself and life in totality. One day, a novel thought entered my consciousness: I was inspired to write a book about my journey of growth, despite experiencing deep challenges and failures. It wouldn't be an exaggeration to say that I'm now living my second life.

This new goal gave me a sense of purpose. It motivated me to live more intentionally. If I complete this goal, I know it will help others by allowing them to progress faster, avoiding the time I wasted figuring it all out. A clearly defined goal provides a roadmap for action and keeps us motivated.

When you have a defined goal, it decides-making quicker and easier because you know where you're headed. After setting the goal of writing and publishing my book to affect and serve my readers, my productivity skyrocketed. I managed my time better and significantly reduced procrastination, which had become my second nature in the absence of a clear goal.

Having defined goals helps you measure your progress and success. These goals are self-made, so there's no external pressure. Achieving small, measurable goals builds confidence and reinforces a sense of accomplishment. Goals are crucial for lifelong learning and personal development—they keep us engaged in productive actions.

When you have a goal, you're less likely to waste time on unproductive activities like daydreaming, getting angry over trivial things, or spending hours on Netflix. These were some of my favorite pastimes when I had no goal. But once I realized the importance of clearly defined goals, everything changed.

Once you've understood the importance of having clear goals, the next step is figuring out how to create goals that set you on a path of progress. Goals that make your life more fulfilling, joyful, and abundant.

Once you've ingrained the belief that clearly defined goals are essential in life, the next step is understanding how to set goals that put you on a path of progress—filling your life with happiness and abundance.

Here are some easy ways to set clearly defined goals for yourself:

1) Identify Your Core Values and Passions

Start by making a list of core values that are non-negotiable for you. These could be things like love, truth, honesty, success, or progress. For example, my core values are love, truth, honesty, success, excellence, and growth—they define who I am at the core. You can open an Excel sheet and write your own core values, along with why they are important to you.

Next, identify your passions. Ask yourself what activities bring you joy and what you are consistently drawn to. This will give you insight into the goals that will resonate deeply with your true self.

2) Know Your Strengths and Areas for Improvement

Understanding your strengths helps you leverage them to achieve your goals. It's important to remember that during the journey of progress, you will face challenges and setbacks. Your strengths will serve as a safety net in tough times.

In my case, I've identified my strengths as:

- Being a sports person, with a passion for Tennis and Table Tennis

- Connecting with people easily through conversations

- Reading to expand my knowledge and satisfy my curiosity

- My family, who is my biggest support system

As for areas of improvement, self-reflection has shown me where I need to grow:

- Managing my thoughts and emotions

- Choosing progress over perfection

- Being happy while pursuing goals

- Cultivating humility and reducing ego

- Becoming a lifelong learner

3) Set SMART Goals

SMART goals are specific, measurable, achievable, relevant, and time-bound:

- **Specific:** Your goals should be clearly defined. When I was struggling as a writer, my goal was specific: to complete and publish my first book.

- **Measurable:** Progress is easier to track when your goals are measurable. Knowing exactly when you'll achieve a goal adds clarity.

- **Achievable:** Goals should challenge you but still be within reach. For instance, becoming a bestselling author with my first book felt unrealistic and added pressure. However, a goal like achieving that status by consistently publishing books is more achievable.

- **Relevant:** Your goals must align with your broader life objectives. My goal of becoming a bestselling author aligns with my desire for time freedom, financial freedom, and the ability to affect others.

- **Time-bound:** Every goal must have a deadline. I set a goal to publish my book within the next two months, which drives me forward with confidence.

4) Visualize Your Ideal Future

Picture your life five, ten, or twenty years from now. What does success look like to you? This mental image serves as a guide, helping you set meaningful goals.

Create a vision board by using images and words that represent your dreams. This visual representation can be a powerful motivator.

5) Seek Feedback and Guidance

The journey to achieving goals can seem long and difficult, but it's traveled one day at a time. Talk to mentors and seek advice from those who have walked the path before you. They can help you avoid mistakes and keep you on track.

Also, keep trying new experiences. They help you grow and gain fresh perspectives that are invaluable for achieving your goals.

6) Regularly Review and Adjust Your Goals

Break down large goals into smaller, manageable steps. This prevents overwhelm and makes progress feel attainable. For example, at work, I was tasked with preparing an Emergency Response and Disaster Management Plan (ERDMP). It felt impossible, but I broke it down into smaller, achievable tasks and worked consistently with my team. We completed the project on time and received recognition for our work.

Always remain flexible and be ready to adapt to your goals as circumstances change. One book that profoundly affected my view on adapting to change Moved *My Cheese?* By Dr. Spencer Johnson. It teaches us to embrace change with a question that stays with me: **"What would you do if you weren't afraid?"**

asked yourself that often—it may lead you to your true path.

- Progress is simple: get up, start small, and set new goals.
- Having goals is very crucial for direction and progress. Not having a goal in life is like being on a ship in an ocean without knowing the final destination.
- Regularly review and adjust your goals according to your present life situations.
- Asked yourself regularly, " what would you do if you were not afraid"

Jot down your thoughts after reading the fourth chapter:

Reflect on the new insights you have gained and apply them to your life situation.

"it does not matter how slowly you go as long as you do not stop"

Confucius

Check if your problem is enormous or you are making it big:

Remember The Alchemist by Paulo Coelho? In the story, the shepherd boy Santiago dreams of finding hidden treasure near the Egyptian pyramids. One day, while resting in an old church near his village with his herd of sheep, he embarks on a long and arduous journey across the desert to reach the pyramids.

Along the way, Santiago encounters various mentors. He learns the art of business from a crystal merchant and befriends an Englishman who is also searching for the elusive alchemist. Eventually, Santiago meets the alchemist, who teaches him the importance of following his unique path in life.

During this journey, Santiago realizes that his veritable treasure isn't found in material wealth but in the growth and learning he gains along the way. However, as Santiago continues his quest, he is confronted by personal doubts and fears about losing everything he holds dear. The alchemist helps him understand that these doubts and fears are natural and integral parts of achieving one's dreams.

When Santiago finally reaches the pyramids, he discovers that the real treasure wasn't a chest of gold. Instead, it was in the lessons he learned throughout his journey. To his surprise, Santiago also finds that the chest of gold he had been searching for was actually buried in the same church where his journey began.

Sometimes, just like Santiago, we all embark on long and difficult journeys, believing that the treasure we seek lies far from home. Yet, more often than not, our real treasure—our answers, our purpose—is closer than we realize, sometimes right in our own surroundings.

I may not know the exact solution to the problems you're facing, but I'm confident that if you inspect around, you'll find that the answers are within your reach.

Embrace progress over Perfection: Story of Linked founder Reid Hoffman

In the early 2000s, Reid Hoffman had a bold vision: to create a platform where professionals could connect, share ideas, and help each other advance in their careers. This idea would eventually become **LinkedIn.**

When Hoffman and his team launched LinkedIn in May 2003, they did so knowing the platform was far from perfect. The interface was clunky, the user base was small, and many doubted whether a professional social network was even necessary.

One of the first major hurdles Hoffman faced was skepticism from potential users and investors. Social networking was still in its infancy, and the idea of connecting with colleagues and strangers online seemed foreign to many. Unlike social platforms like Friendster and MySpace, LinkedIn wasn't built for fun—it was for work, and many questioned whether people would ever embrace it.

Hoffman knew that waiting for a perfect product could mean missing a critical **window of opportunity**. Instead, he launched early, with a basic version that would allow real users to test the platform and provide feedback. This decision was risky; the initial version of LinkedIn had many flaws, and the team was often embarrassed by its limitations.

But instead of seeing these flaws as failures, Hoffman viewed them as opportunities for progress. He embraced a philosophy of continuous iteration, where the focus was on learning and improving rather than achieving perfection from the start. For example, one of LinkedIn's early challenges was user growth. The platform initially struggled to attract members, with only 20 sign-ups on the first day.

This could have been discouraging for many, but Hoffman and his team used the slow start to refine their approach. They add new features like the "Import Contacts" tool, which made it easier for users to invite their networks, and introduced the "Groups" feature, which allowed professionals to connect to shared interests.

Another significant challenge was monetization. Investors were eager to see returns, but Hoffman knew that rushing to implement a revenue model could alienate users and stifle growth. Instead, he focused on building a strong, engaged community first, believing that progress in this area would eventually lead to sustainable profits. This strategy paid off—by the time LinkedIn introduced premium subscriptions and job postings, it had already become an indispensable tool for professionals, making monetization easier and more effective.

Hoffman's choice to prioritize progress over perfection allowed LinkedIn to develop rapidly. By constantly iterating, the platform could adapt to user needs and stay ahead of competitors. Each hurdle, whether it was slow user adoption or uncertainty about the business model, became an opportunity to learn and improve.

Hoffman's willingness to **launch an imperfect product** and focus on incremental progress was a major life-changing decision, not only for him but for the millions of professionals who now rely on LinkedIn for their careers.

Today, LinkedIn is the world's largest professional network, with over 900 million members in over 200 countries. Reid Hoffman's journey with LinkedIn is a powerful example of how choosing progress over perfection can lead to extraordinary success. It's a testament to the idea that waiting for the perfect moment or perfect product can sometimes mean missing out entirely. By embracing imperfection and focusing on constant growth, Hoffman turned his vision into a global phenomenon that continues to shape the professional world.

The power of kaizen: Continuous improvements bring significant results in the long run.

Masaaki Imai's journey began in post-war Japan, where he grew up witnessing the country's struggles to rebuild after the devastation of World War II. In 1955, at just 25 years old, he started working at the **Japan Productivity Center,** where he observed that traditional management techniques focused on dramatic overhauls rather than steady improvements. This realization led him to embrace Kaizen, a Japanese philosophy meaning "continuous improvement." Throughout the 1960s, Imai applied Kaizen to his own life, making small, consistent changes that significantly enhanced his productivity and personal growth.

In 1975, he founded the Kaizen Institute, which is dedicated to helping companies implement this powerful philosophy, which has already transformed Toyota into a global leader in efficiency and quality.

By 1986, Imai's ideas gained international recognition with the publication of his book, "Kaizen: The Key to Japan's Competitive Success," which introduced the world to the concept of Kaizen. The book became a bestseller, and organizations worldwide began adopting Kaizen to drive efficiency and innovation. Throughout the 1990s and beyond, Imai travelled the globe, spreading the principles of Kaizen across various industries. His work had a profound impact, not only on businesses but also on individuals who embraced the mindset of continuous improvement. Today, Kaizen remains a global standard for success, and Imai's legacy endures as a testament to the power of progress over perfection.

The Book of Progress: Mastery by Robert Greene

After a long-cherished holiday in the Maldives with my wife, I landed at Delhi Airport, feeling joyful and inspired. We visited Connaught Place for some shopping, and there, in an old bookshop called Jain Book Agency, I stumbled upon an incredible book—**Mastery** by Robert Greene.

This book is an extraordinary read, guiding you through the life journeys of individuals who discovered their "ikigai" and pinpointed their true calling. Greene introduces readers to the lives of great achievers like Leonardo da Vinci, Charles Darwin, Benjamin Franklin, Mozart, Michael Faraday, Albert Einstein, Thomas Edison, the Wright Brothers, and many more. The book details the processes these remarkable individuals followed to find their paths and overcome challenges common on the road to mastery.

Why am I sharing this? Because this book had a profound impact on changing my thought pattern from "I've lost it all forever" to "I can still win." It gave me hope, showing that the path to greatness is filled with difficulties—something everyone goes through. My extreme pain, rooted in the belief that I had lost everything, began transforming into an inspirational quest for progress and success.

Mastery inspired me to find my path and unlock my full potential. I started reading out of curiosity, developing a habit of exploring a wide range of topics—personal growth, overcoming challenges, mastery of human emotions, excellence, and achievement. Non-fiction books became my companions on this journey.

Around 2018, a natural desire surfaced within me to write a book and share my teachings with others who might face similar challenges. The idea was to shorten the period of struggle for my readers. It had taken me seven to eight years to start my journey back on the road to progress and growth. For those years, I was only putting in 60% effort, just dragging along. I wanted to help others get back on track quickly, to restart their journey with no time lost after a setback or major hurdle.

As we know, "the entire universe conspires to fulfill the desire of a person who wants to do something with devotion." One day, while browsing Instagram, I came across a course on writing and publishing books. It intrigued me, so I enrolled. This was a significant step forward for me—it put me back on the path of growth and success, and I started rediscovering the powers I thought I had lost forever.

The book you are reading is a living proof of the powerful ideas which I am sharing with you, so that you may start your journey of freedom and progress.

Important points from fifth chapter:

- Check if you are unnecessarily making your problems big. Often solutions are near to you or are within you. You just need to be open to receive them.
- Embrace progress over perfection. This shit in mindset will bring peace and fulfillment in your daily working.
- Experience the power of Kaizen: Continuous improvement brings significant results in the long run.

Jot down your thoughts after reading the fifth chapter

Reflect on the new insights you have gained and apply them to your life situation.

Chapter 6- Novel methods of progress

" if you want something you have never had, you must do something you have never done "

Thomas Jefferson

Convert pain into strength: Mahatma Ghandi India (

Customizing your progress)

While I share with your time-tested methods—pathways followed by prominent leaders and organizations to progress and move forward in life—I also want to remind you of a great truth. The strongest progress radar that will guide your growth is always within you. The greatest power that will show you the way forward is already inside you.

Consider the journey of Mahatma Gandhi after his return to India from South Africa in 1915. He had spent over 20 years fighting against racial discrimination there, developing his philosophy of non-violent resistance, *Satyagraha*. By the time he returned to India, Gandhi was already a well-known figure, but his fight for India's independence had only just begun.

For the next 15 years, Gandhi's struggle was rooted in non-violence—a concept completely foreign to the British rulers of India. One of the most oppressive laws imposed by the British was the Salt Act, which prohibited Indians from making or selling salt, forcing them to buy it from British suppliers. Salt, a basic necessity for the poor, had now become a symbol of exploitation.

Even after years of dedicated effort, Gandhi hadn't yet made the impact. He was a man of resilience, though. Instead of working within existing frameworks, he operated from the heart. Moved deeply by the suffering caused by the salt laws, Gandhi went into deep introspection. He realized that to uproot the British, something new and unique had to be done.

Then, an idea struck him. What if he used the very law that was causing so much pain to unite Indians and attract global attention? And so, on March 12, 1930, Gandhi embarked on the historic Dandi March—a 24-day, 240-mile journey from Sabarmati Ashram to the coastal village of Dandi in Gujarat. What began with 78 followers soon grew into a massive movement, with thousands of people joining him along the way.

On April 6, 1930, Gandhi reached Dandi and symbolically broke the Salt Law by picking up a lump of salt from the seashore. ***He says, "With this, I am shaking the foundations of the British Empire."*** This simple act of defiance became a turning point in India's independence movement. Even though 60,000 Indians, including Gandhi, were arrested, the Salt Satyagraha became an international news story, showing the world the power of non-violent resistance.

Gandhi's ability to think outside of the traditional framework and his resilience are a source of inspiration for all of us. The Dandi March reignited hope in a time of complete darkness. It united the nation, and for the first time, everyone believed freedom was near.

This story is a reminder that, just like Gandhi, we have a radar inside us that will guide us through our toughest challenges. Trust it. The answers you seek are within you.

Know that you do not know: Learn to unlearn

Often, with age and routine success in our daily work, we become rigid, believing we know it all. We make the mistake of thinking we are better than others simply because we study at a well-ranked college or have a higher-paying job. In doing so, we become our own worst enemies, limiting our growth and shutting ourselves off from new opportunities.

Albert Einstein: Embracing the Unknown

His journey to success was deeply rooted in his ability to acknowledge what he did not know. Early in his career, Einstein faced challenges in academia, often questioning the established theories of physics.

He famously unlearned the classical Newtonian concepts that dominated the field and embraced the unknown by exploring the possibilities of space, time, and energy in new ways.

Einstein's openness to possibilities and willingness to challenge the status quo led him to develop the theory of relativity, revolutionizing our understanding of the universe. His work earned him the Nobel Prize in Physics in 1921 and changed the course of science forever. Einstein's success shows that progress often comes from recognizing the limits of our knowledge and exploring beyond them. You may realise that he lived by this truth day in and day out to always look at things with new possibilities.

"The more I learn, the more I realize how much I don't know."- Einstein

This quote encapsulates Einstein's deep understanding that pursuiting knowledge often reveals the vastness of what remains unknown, emphasizing his lifelong curiosity and openness to new ideas.

Steve Jobs: Unlearning to Innovate

Steve Jobs, co-founder of Apple, is another powerful example of someone who succeeded by embracing the idea that "you do not know" everything.

When Apple was developing the iPhone, Jobs insisted on rethinking the traditional mobile phone design.

Rather than following the conventional approach of adding more buttons or features, Jobs envisioned a device with a simple, intuitive touch interface. This required unlearning what was known about mobile phone design at the time and opening up to the possibility of something radically different. The iPhone's success redefined the mobile industry and solidified Apple's place as a leader in innovation.

Akio Morita: Sony's belief in their unique idea

Akio Morita, co-founder of Sony, was instrumental in the development of products that revolutionized the electronics industry. One of Sony's most famous innovations, the **Walkman**, came from Morita's willingness to look beyond existing knowledge and market research, which at the time suggested there was no demand for a portable music player.

Morita went with his gut feeling. He embraced the unknown possibilities and pushed forward with the Walkman's development, believing in its potential to change how people listened to music.

The Walkman became a global phenomenon, demonstrating that **progress often comes from**

questioning and unlearning established market assumptions.

Marie Curie: Exploring the Unseen

Marie Curie, a pioneering physicist and chemist, was the first woman to win a Nobel Prize and remains the only person to have won Nobel Prizes in two different sciences (Physics and Chemistry). Curie's groundbreaking work on radioactivity was possible because she will explore what was unknown and uncharted.

When the properties of radioactive elements were not fully understood, Curie investigated these unknowns, challenging the existing knowledge in physics and chemistry. Her relentless pursuit of understanding the unknown led to the discovery of radium and polonium, transforming the scientific community's understanding of atomic science and paving the way for future research in nuclear physics.

These stories highlight how major success often comes not from a quest for perfection, but from the courage to acknowledge what we do not know, to unlearn old ways, and to explore new possibilities. Embracing this mindset allows for progress that is flexible, innovative, and transformative.

Be your Biggest Supporter: Start believing in yourself
(*Golden Power*)

No amount of knowledge or wisdom will ever help you if you don't learn to implement the wisdom I'm about to share.

No love from friends or family will matter if you don't know how to love yourself. No amount of money or luxury—no matter how many resources you have—will be of any use if you're not able to tap into your own unlimited source of abundance. No fleeting joy from socializing, listening to your favorite music, or attending endless parties will bring you lasting happiness and fulfillment.

So, what is this wisdom for personal growth that stands above all others?

The wisdom is this: **You have to be your biggest supporter and your deepest believer in the entire world.**

Remember this always. Write it down and stick it on the wall in front of you.

Malala Yousafzai's story: (She was her biggest believer)

Born in 1997 in the Swat Valley of Pakistan, Malala grew up in an environment where the Taliban frequently targeted girls' education. Despite the increasing danger, Malala was determined to pursue her education and began writing a blog under a pseudonym for the BBC in 2009, at just 11 years old, describing life under Taliban rule and advocating for girls' rights to education. Her outspokenness made her a target, and in October 2012, at 15, she was shot in the head by a Taliban gunman while riding the bus home from school. Remarkably, she survived and was flown to the UK for treatment.

Instead of succumbing to fear, Malala's self-belief grew even stronger. In 2013, she co-authored the memoir I Am Malala, which detailed her journey and her fight for girls' education. The book became an international bestseller, further amplifying her voice. That same year, she spoke at the United Nations on her 16th birthday, calling for worldwide access to education. Her advocacy continued to gain momentum, and in 2014, at 17, Malala became the youngest-ever recipient of the Nobel Peace Prize.

In 2017, she was accepted to study Philosophy, Politics, and Economics at the University of Oxford, furthering her education while continuing her global advocacy. Throughout her journey, Malala has faced immense challenges—being targeted by extremists, living in exile, and navigating the pressures of global recognition at a young age. Yet, she remained her own biggest supporter, never doubting the power of her voice and her mission. Her story inspires millions around the world to believe in themselves, even in the face of the most daunting challenges, and to stand firm in pursuiting their goals.

Oprah Winfrey's Story: (She was her biggest believer)

One story that encapsulates Oprah Winfrey's incredible willpower and belief in herself is the moment she produced and star in the movie The Color Purple.

In 1985, Oprah was still relatively unknown, working as a local talk show host in Chicago. She had read Alice Walker's novel The Colour Purple and felt a deep connection with the story, which resonated with her own experiences of adversity and triumph. When she learned that Steven Spielberg was adapting the book into a movie, Oprah was determined to be a part of it, even though she had no acting experience and had never been in a major film.

Oprah auditioned for the role of Sofia, but after weeks of waiting and not hearing, she began to doubt herself. During this period, she attended a weight-loss camp to manage her stress and anxiety. While there, Oprah received a call that would change her life. She was offered the role of Sofia in The Color Purple.

Overcome with emotion, Oprah realized that her unwavering belief in herself and her determination to be part of the project had paid off. Despite her lack of acting experience and the challenges she faced, Oprah's performance was so powerful that it earned her an Academy Award nomination for Best Supporting Actress.

This moment is a defining example of Oprah's willpower and self-belief. She took a massive leap of faith in pursuing a role that seemed beyond her reach, and her conviction not only changed the course of her career but also introduced her to a global audience. Oprah's belief in her own potential, even when the odds were against her, is a testament to the power of being your biggest supporter.

Consistent Imperfect Action: Do not wait for perfection, strive for excellence.

When you take consistent imperfect action, several key processes occur in the brain that facilitate progress and growth. Have a look at what happens inside your brain when you take consistent imperfect action.

1. Neuroplasticity Activation

Neuroplasticity- refers to the brain's ability to reorganize itself by forming new neural connections. When you engage in consistent, imperfect actions, you are repeatedly activating and refining neural pathways associated with the task. This repeated practice helps in strengthening these pathways, making it easier for the brain to perform and improve the skill. For instance, practicing a new skill like coding or playing an instrument builds and refines the relevant neural circuits, enhancing proficiency.

2. Learning and Memory Formation

Learning involves encoding new information and skills into memory. When you take consistent actions, even if they are not perfect, your brain processes and stores the experiences. This incremental learning helps in refining techniques and strategies. The hippocampus, a key brain region involved in forming recent memories, plays a crucial role here. The more you practice and adjust your approach, the more robust your memory and understanding of the task become, leading to progress.

3. Error-Driven Learning

The brain uses *error signals* to adapt and improve. When you make mistakes, the brain's error-detection system (involving areas such as the anterior cingulate cortex) helps you analyze what went wrong. This process of reflecting on errors and making corrections enhances learning. Consistent practice with imperfections allows the brain to learn from these mistakes and make necessary adjustments, leading to gradual improvement and mastery.

4. Cognitive Flexibility

Cognitive flexibility is the brain's ability to adapt to new information and changing circumstances. Taking consistent, imperfect actions requires you to continually adjust your strategies and approaches based on feedback and results. This process helps in developing cognitive flexibility, which is essential for problem-solving and adapting to new challenges. As you refine your approach to practice, cognitive flexibility increases, facilitating better adaptation and progress.

5. Motivation and Reward System

The brain's *reward system*, including structures like the nucleus accumbens and ventral tegmental area, is activated by achieving goals and making progress. Even small successes and improvements provide a sense of reward, reinforcing continued effort. Consistent actions, even when imperfect, create frequent opportunities for these small rewards, boosting motivation and encouraging further effort. This positive feedback loop supports ongoing engagement and progress.

When you take consistent, imperfect actions, several key brain processes support progress:

Neuroplasticity strengthens and refines neural pathways.

Learning and memory formation enhance skill acquisition.

Error-driven learning helps analyze and correct mistakes.

Cognitive flexibility improves adaptability and problem-solving.

Motivation and reward systems reinforce continued effort.

So make it your **Brain tattoo**, that Consistent imperfect action is the most potent weapon for growth and progress.

Together, these processes facilitate steady progress and skill development, showing that imperfection is a valuable component of growth and success.

Start Using the tool of creative Visualization:

1. Define Your Goal:

Clearly identify what you want to achieve. Be specific about your goal, whether it's a personal aspiration, a career milestone, or a skill you want to develop.

2. Find a Quiet Space:

Choose a calm and comfortable environment where you can focus without interruptions. This could be a quiet room, a peaceful park, or a cozy corner in your home.

3. Relax and Breathe:

Take a few deep breaths to calm your mind and body. Relaxation helps you enter a more receptive state for visualization.

4. Visualize Clearly:

Close your eyes and create a detailed mental image of your goal. Imagine achieving it, **including the sights, sounds, and feelings associated with success**. Make the visualization as vivid and realistic as possible.

5. Engage Your Emotions:

Feel the emotions you would experience upon achieving your goal. Whether it's excitement, joy, or pride, engaging with these **emotions strengthens** the visualization's impact.

6. Repeat Regularly:

Practice visualization daily or as often as possible. Consistency helps reinforce your mental image and keeps your focus on your goal.

7. Affirm and Act:

Combine visualization with positive affirmations that support your goal. Follow up with concrete actions towards achieving your goal, as visualization alone is not enough.

Why we should do Creative Visualization?

Clarifies Goals: Visualization helps you clearly define and understand your goals.

Boosts Motivation: Imagining success can enhance your motivation and drive to take action.

Enhances Focus: Regular visualization helps maintain focus on your goals amidst distractions.

Builds Confidence: Seeing yourself succeed mentally builds confidence and reduces anxiety about real-life challenges.

When will you start seeing the results of creative visualization?

Short-Term: In the short term, you may notice increased motivation, clarity, and a sense of direction. Visualization can help you stay focused and motivated to start taking actionable steps.

Medium-Term: Over a few weeks to months, you may observe improved confidence and progress toward your goals as you take more purposeful actions.

Long-Term: With consistent practice, you could achieve significant milestones and see tangible results. Visualization helps align your mindset and actions with your goals, leading to long-term success.

Examples from Famous People

1. Michael Phelps: The Olympic swimmer used creative visualization techniques to prepare for races. He would visualize every detail of his races, including potential challenges, and mentally rehearse his performance. This practice contributed to his record-breaking success and many gold medals.

2. Jim Carrey: The actor famously wrote himself a check for $10 million for "acting services rendered" dated for Thanksgiving 1995. He kept the check in his wallet and visualized himself receiving such an amount. By 1994, Carrey received a role in Dumb and Dumber that paid him $10 million, demonstrating the power of visualization.

3. Oprah Winfrey: Oprah used creative visualization techniques throughout her career. She often visualized her success and personal growth, which helped her achieve her goals and become a media mogul and philanthropist.

Creative visualization is a powerful tool for personal and professional growth. By consistently practicing it, you can enhance your focus and motivation, and ultimately achieve your goals.

Along with creative visualization, you may start listening to music, which uplifts your spirit and keeps you going for the day.

1. Enhances Focus and Productivity

Detailed Mechanism:

Music's Effect on Brain Activity: Music can increase dopamine levels, which improve mood and concentration. Instrumental music or music with a steady rhythm can help filter out distractions, enabling better focus on tasks.

Ludwig van Beethoven, despite his hearing loss, composed some of his most renowned works by immersing himself in music. His ability to focus on composition despite personal challenges exemplifies how music can aid in maintaining concentration and productivity.

2. Boosts Motivation and Performance

Music and Physical Endurance: Upbeat and high-tempo music can elevate heart rate and reduce perceived effort, making physical tasks, such as exercise, feel less strenuous and more enjoyable.

Eliud Kipchoge- Kenyan marathon runner Eliud Kipchoge, while not listening to music during races, has used music in training to boost motivation and performance. Music helps him maintain a steady rhythm and enhances his stamina during long training sessions.

3. Reduces Stress and Enhances Relaxation

Music and Cortisol Levels: Listening to relaxing music can lower cortisol levels, reducing stress and promoting a calm state. This can enhance overall well-being and improve performance in stressful situations.

Dr. Oliver Sacks: Renowned neurologist Dr. Oliver Sacks documented how music therapy helped patients with neurological disorders manage stress and anxiety. In his book Music philia, he explores how music can be a therapeutic tool for reducing stress and aiding relaxation.

4. Fosters Creativity and Innovation

Music and Creative Thinking: Certain types of music, particularly ambient or classical music, can create a conducive environment for creativity by reducing mental clutter and enhancing cognitive flexibility.

Steve Jobs: Steve Jobs often used music to stimulate his creativity. He was known for his affinity for classic music and its role in his thought process. Jobs' innovative approach to Apple was partly fuelled by his ability to use music to enhance creative thinking and problem-solving.

Improves Social Connection and Teamwork

Music and Social Bonding: Shared musical experiences, such as singing or playing instruments together, can strengthen social bonds and improve teamwork. Music can create a sense of unity and collective motivation.

Glee Club Impact: The Glee Club phenomenon in schools and communities has shown how music fosters teamwork and social connections. For example, schools with active Glee Club report improved student morale and collaboration, demonstrating how music enhances social dynamics and collective progress.

The WIN Concept: Michael Phelps' Golden Path

In the bustling arena of global swimming, Michael Phelps was already a name whispered in awe. But behind the scenes, a simple yet profound principle shaped his journey to becoming the most decorated Olympian of all time. It was called the "WIN" concept, a guiding philosophy that stands for "**What's Important Now?**"

Phelps' coach, Bob Bowman, introduced the concept early in his career. It wasn't about winning medals or breaking records, but about staying laser-focused on the present moment. In training, Phelps would ask himself, "What's Important Now?" Was it nailing a perfect turn, keeping his form, or maintaining his breathing rhythm? Each day, each stroke, was a step closer to greatness because he prioritized the small, critical actions that mattered most at that very instant.

This mindset wasn't just about training. It was about life. When Phelps faced personal challenges, like his battles with anxiety and depression, the WIN concept kept him anchored. Rather than letting the weight of his past or the pressure of future expectations overwhelm him, he would focus on the here and now. Whether it was reaching out for help, stepping back from the spotlight, or just taking a deep breath, Phelps made choices that aligned with what was important in that moment.

During races, especially in the pressure-cooker atmosphere of the Olympics, Phelps' ability to focus on "What's Important Now?" was his superpower. Instead of being distracted by the noise, the competitors, or even the clock, he honed in on the exact moment—the feel of the water, the power in his strokes, the finish line that was just a fingertip away.

The WIN concept wasn't about perfection; it was about progress. Every choice Phelps made, big or small, was a piece of the larger puzzle. It allowed him to stay present, to push forward, and ultimately, to become a legend. His story is a testament to the power of focusing on "What's Important Now" and choosing progress over the illusion of perfection.

Important points from sixth chapter:

- Convert your pain into strength, change your perspective about challenge, read more about the solutions for the challenge. Start taking it as an opportunity for growth.
- Know that "you do not know". Be completely open to new knowledge. It is an enormous power.
- Believe in your unique ideas. Keep exploring the unknown. Back your ideas when nobody believes in the idea. People are accustomed to reject new ideas.
- Always be your biggest supporter. Have faith in your abilities, always back yourself. Whatever happens, always be your biggest supporter. *This is the Golden power.*
- Take consistent imperfect action. Do not wait for perfection, strive for excellence.
- Start using the tool of creative visualisation.
- Add Music to your life. It makes us more happy and more focussed.
- WIN: Live by the "WIN" principal, always do what is important now. Make it your *brain tattoo.*

Jot down your thoughts after reading the sixth chapter

Reflect on the new insights you have gained and apply them to your life situation.

" success is not the key to happiness. Happiness is the key to success. If you love what you are doing, you will be successful"

Albert Schweitzer

Learn to be joyful while you are chasing your Goals

Dear reader, as you embark on pursuiting any dream, always keep the end in mind. Whatever we chase in life, whether it's running a successful business, earning that coveted Ivy League degree, winning an Olympic medal, or publishing an international best-selling book, at its core, we are seeking one thing: happiness and fulfilment.

Many of us believe that achieving these dreams will bring us closer to our true selves, to a state of eternal joy. But here's a question to consider: If all we are truly chasing is happiness, why wait until we reach our goals to feel it? Why not commit to being joyful *today*, in every step of the journey?

The key lies in making a few fundamental shifts in our mindset. Once we realize that the journey itself holds the potential for happiness, we free ourselves from the burden of waiting for a distant outcome to feel fulfilled. True joy comes not just from the destination, but from the process of getting there.

By embracing this, we can create a life where happiness is part of our daily routine, no matter how far we are from our goal.

Leonardo da Vinci: The Renaissance Polymath's Love for Learning

Leonardo da Vinci is celebrated as one of history's greatest geniuses, known for his contributions to art, science, and engineering. However, what truly set Leonardo apart was his insatiable curiosity and love for learning. He didn't just paint masterpieces like the "Mona Lisa" or "The Last Supper"; he approached every project with a **deep sense of wonder and joy.**

Leonardo's notebooks are filled with sketches, observations, and ideas on topics ranging from anatomy to flight. He often left his works unfinished, not out of negligence, but because he was more interested in exploring new ideas than in completing a task for its own sake. His joy came from the process of discovery and creation, rather than the accolades or recognition.

This approach not only made Leonardo a master of multiple disciplines, but also allowed him to live a life filled with continuous learning and exploration.

Lesson: Leonardo da Vinci's life shows that pursuiting knowledge and the joy of exploration can lead to unparalleled creativity and fulfilment.

Matsuo Bashō: The Joy of the Journey in Haiku

Matsuo Bashō, Japan's most famous haiku poet, found profound joy in the simple act of wandering through the Japanese countryside. Bashō believed that life itself was a journey, and his poetry reflected the beauty and transience of each moment he experienced along the way.

Bashō's most famous work, "The Narrow Road to the Deep North," is not just a travelogue but a reflection of the joy he found in the journey itself. As he traveled, he composed haiku that captured the essence of fleeting moments—a frog jumping into a pond, the moon shining over the fields. His joy came from being present in the moment and appreciating the minor details of life.

Bashō's poetry, rooted in the journey's joy, has left an indelible mark on Japanese literature and continues to inspire people around the world to find beauty in the everyday.

Lesson: Matsuo Bashō's life and work remind us that true fulfillment comes from being present and finding joy in the simple moments along life's journey.

Albert Einstein: The Playfulness of Discovery

Albert Einstein, one of the most brilliant minds in history, approached his work with a sense of curiosity and playfulness that is often overlooked. Einstein's theory of relativity revolutionized our understanding of the universe, but it was his joy in the process of discovery that truly defined his life.

Einstein once says, "I have no special talent. I am only passionately curious." He viewed his scientific work as play, a way to explore the mysteries of the universe with a childlike sense of wonder. Whether he was contemplating light or the fabric of space-time, Einstein found joy in the questions themselves, not just the answers.

This playful approach to learning and discovery not only led to groundbreaking theories, but also made Einstein one of the most beloved and inspiring figures in the history of science.

Lesson: Albert Einstein's life shows that approaching your work with curiosity and a sense of play can lead to extraordinary discoveries and a deeply fulfilling life.

Commit to Be cheerful and playful the whole day

For those of you who have journeyed with me through this book, you already understand that our choices shape our future. In the same way, whether we fall into a cycle of sadness, victimhood, and fear, or choose to be cheerful, playful, and committed to seeing the surrounding good — to see the world through the eyes of a child full of wonder and possibility — it all comes down to one simple thing: the choices we make.

So, what choice will you make? Will you choose to be joyful, or will you let yourself be consumed by sadness and gloom?

The wisdom of understanding that *it is our choice* is incredibly powerful. Once we grasp this truth, it becomes a matter of willpower to practice it daily. Yes, it will require effort, but once you begin to experience the rewards, you'll realize this is one of the greatest powers you possess. The choice is always yours.

Science supports this idea as well. Many studies show that happier people are more productive and achieve more in life compared to those who are consistently sad or negative. Happiness is not just a feeling — it's a powerful tool that can propel you forward in all areas of life.

Lesson from Indian Yogi Sadhguru: "If You Have One Eye on the Goal, Only One Eye is Left for Finding the Way"

As I was reading a book by Swami Vivekananda, he beautifully compared our human condition to that of honeybees. We enter this world to live fully and freely, but often, we get trapped in the clutter of our own goals. We set these goals intending to achieve freedom, yet more often than not, we find ourselves stuck in the web we've spun — much like a honeybee that comes to sip from the pot of honey, only to get its hands and feet stuck.

I'm sure many of you can relate. Maybe you made a brilliant plan to pursue an MBA from a prestigious institute, but now you're struggling to find your correct direction. Or perhaps you married the most suitable partner, only to face life's tough questions afterward. Or you started a new business, full of confidence and a desire to change the world, only to discover there's so much more to figure out along the way.

How did our goals and achievements become more important than life itself?

At a student conference at Harvard Kennedy School, a student once asked Sadhguru, the founder of Isha Foundation, how one can follow the essential teaching of the Bhagavad Gita — to work sincerely without being attached to the results. Sadhguru's answer was profound: Krishna himself was deeply committed to marrying the spiritual process with the political process, and he was intensely working towards results.

Sadhguru clarified goals are merely there to give us direction. Once we understand this, the real focus should be on the means — the small, hourly, daily, and weekly tasks we undertake. Obsessing over the goal can blur our vision, leading to distraction or even disaster. He says, "If you have one eye fixed on the goal, you have only one eye left to find your way," and that makes the journey inefficient.

Think about it. If I want to drive to a destination 500 kilometers away, but keep thinking about the end point, I'm likely to hit another car or cyclist along the way because my vision is clouded by my fixation on the goal.

Most of you reading this book are intellectuals and educated beings. I believe this knowledge will resonate deeply with you. It's one of the oldest, most fundamental truths to achieving goals: focus on the process, not the outcome. There is no other way.

To be honest, I recently came across this insight myself and have practiced it consciously. By keeping both eyes on the path, I know I'll reach the destination.

Once you discover your true love, your passion, you'll start enjoying the process. That's the whole point.

This truth has been echoed by many talented individuals:

1. **Serena Williams**: "The love I have for tennis keeps me going, even on the toughest days. It's that passion that fuels my desire to keep improving and give everything I have on the court."

2. **J. K. Rowling**: "Writing has always been my true love. It's the passion for storytelling that kept me going through rejection after rejection, and it's what still drives me today."

3. **Michael Jordan**: "Basketball was my true love. That love pushed me to practice, to compete, and to never give up, no matter the challenges."

4. **Oprah Winfrey**: "My passion for connecting with people and telling their stories drives me. It's that love for what I do that has kept me going throughout my career."

5. **Elon Musk**: "The love for what I do, whether it's building rockets or cars, is what drives me. Without that deep passion, none of the successes would have been possible."

Now, as a manager, I manage things to make a living — I decide, communicate through emails, delegate tasks, and upgrade my skills through training. I use technology to generate reports that aid decision-making. If I love what I do, that's wonderful. But if I don't, it's important to ask myself, "What is it I don't like? And what can I do about it?" Learning to love what you do is the secret to success. If you can't, then seek roles and tasks that align with what you love.

Finally, I feel blessed and amazed by the power of embracing the incomplete. It is this very realization that has made it possible for the book you are reading to finally become a reality. This dream had been incomplete for the last six years, and it would have remained so if not for the divine guidance of Lord Ram, Hanuman, and Maa Saraswati, who showed me that "embracing the incomplete" is, in fact, my greatest strength. All I needed was to shift my perspective and see it not as a challenge, but as a gift.

Like me, I know you too have many incomplete goals and desires. Now, pick the one that has been your most cherished dream and start working on it again. Remember, incompleteness is nothing but the last step before you achieve that desire.

Unique and Novel Ideas to Achieve Your Goals Without Pressure:

1. **Do every task with joy**

    Approach everything you do with happiness and
    enthusiasm. When you're joyful, asks no longer feel
    like burdens, and you naturally progress toward
    your goals.

2. **Never aim to 'complete' the goal**

    Forget about the outcome. Learn to love the
    process. Focus on the steps, the means, and the
    journey. Your destination is inevitable when you do
    this—you will arrive.

3. **Be like Captain Cool—M.S. Dhoni**

    Take inspiration from Mahendra Singh Dhoni's
    calmness and presence of mind. Don't let stress
    about the result cloud your focus. Stay relaxed, like
    Dhoni on the cricket field, and everything will fall
    into place.

4. **Wisdom from Sadhguru (Indian Yogi)**
    Sadhguru often talks about how Krishna balanced
    spirituality and politics for the greater good.
    Krishna advised Arjuna to focus on his duty and let
    go of worrying about the outcome, because life
    itself is uncertain and death could come at any
    moment. This teaches us that life is about giving
    our best to the present moment, without
    attachment to the result

Swami Vivekananda says, "Once your goals are set, forget
them. Commit wholeheartedly to the process, putting all
your energy and focus into the work at hand." The result,

he believed, is inevitable because of the greater universal law of cause and effect. The work you do today is the cause, and the results will naturally follow as the effect. This concept is echoed in Newton's Third Law of Motion: *For every action, there is an equal and opposite reaction.* Just as no force in nature goes unanswered, no effort you make goes unrewarded. When you invest your energy, the universe responds in kind, and the result becomes a certainty, not a question.

Imagine this—every small step you take, every imperfect action you make, sets off a ripple in the universe. The result may not be visible immediately, but it is forming, growing, and moving toward you with equal force. That's the power of committing to the process.

Now, let this knowledge sink in: your incomplete goals are not failures; they are simply waiting for your next step. Begin today without worrying about the outcome. Commit with joy to the journey, and trust the universal law that what you seek is already on its way to you.

So, as you move forward, know this: *The only thing between you and your goal is your next action.*

I encourage you to embrace incompleteness as a powerful tool. It is not a sign of failure, but of growth and progress. Once you understand this, you'll see that what feels incomplete is simply on its way to becoming complete.

Important points from seventh chapter:
- Learn to enjoy while you are chasing your goals.

- Be committed to cheerfulness and playfulness every single day.
- " If you have one eye on the goal, you are left with only one eye to find your way"- Sadhguru.
- Be committed to enjoy the process of growth and progress.

Conclusion:

In this hyper-competitive world, where achievements and goals have taken precedence over the overall happiness and wellbeing of humans, it is important to look at the entire process of defining goals and achieving them from a new perspective.

We need to look at why we get stuck in our goals and refine our goals regarding our "why".

We need to find our "why" and redefine our goals around it. It will help us find true satisfaction and help us live a meaningful life filled with purpose and fulfilment.

Always remember whatever is your current situation, however bad it seems to you. There is always a solution and a way to progress, a way to start afresh and new, a way to progress and happiness.

I am sharing a few practical ways to start living a life of progress and fulfilment.

Practice them and start living a life of freedom and abundance.

1. Most of the times your solution lies in the challenges you are facing. You just need to change your perspective about the challenge.

2. It is possible to convert your greatest weakness into your greatest strength.

3. Perfectionism is a hurdle on your path of progress. Choose progress over perfection.

4. Do not let your past rule over your present. Be free in the present to create a future of abundance and freedom.

5. It is always possible to start a fresh even if you are feeling completely defeated, broken, ruined and lost forever. Be inspired by the story of the mysterious bird Phoenix, which always rises from its ashes.

6. Practice Shoshin (Beginner's mind): To start all tasks with a beginner's mind. Always curious, happy to learn, always enthusiastic, free from the past, joyfully present, always open to all possibilities, to lead a life of progress and eternal growth. Shoshin protects us from the burden of experience and stress of being an expert.

7. Recognise the pit of procrastination: Fear of failure, going for perfection, lack of motivation and indecisiveness leads you to procrastination.

8. Check Are You Tied to a Small Rope Like the Elephant?

9. Break away your ropes of limiting beliefs and start to think freely. Transform your limiting beliefs into powerful thoughts of freedom.

10. Match your skills with your goals for enjoying the flow of living.

11. Check whether your ego is your friend or your enemy.

12. Check if you need a mentor on your journey. Role of a suitable mentor is crucial on the path of progress.

13. Find your "why", write it down, practice reading it every day before you sleep. Your "why" is your

North start, which gives purpose and direction to life.

14. Small daily wins give you much required momentum for consistent progress in life.

15. Growth mindset: The belief that abilities and intelligence can be developed through consistent effort, learning, and perseverance. Practice a growth mindset to overcome any challenge by developing new skills and abilities.

16. Grit: Perseverance and passion play a much greater role in success as compared to other factors, like intellectual capabilities. It is not the most intelligent, but the most determined who is more likely to succeed in the long run.

17. Learn to embrace the "messy middle", a period of frustration, failure and rejection before you taste the sweet success.

18. Brain is a dynamic and ever changing system. So it is always possible to rewire our brains, at any stage of life, that will help to progress faster.

19. Progress is simple: get up, start small, and set new goals.

20. Having goals is very crucial for direction and progress. Not having a goal in life is like being on a ship in an ocean without knowing the final destination.

21. Regularly review and adjust your goals according to your present life situations.

22. Asked yourself regularly, " what would you do if you were not afraid"

23. Check if you are unnecessarily making your problems big. Often solutions are near to you or are within you. You just need to be open to receive them.

24. Embrace progress over perfection. This shit in mindset will bring peace and fulfillment in your daily working.

25. Experience the power of Kaizen: Continuous improvement brings significant results in the long run.

26. Convert your pain into strength, change your perspective about challenge, read more about the solutions for the challenge. Start taking it as an opportunity for growth.

27. Know that "you do not know". Be completely open to new knowledge. It is an enormous power.

28. Believe in your unique ideas. Keep exploring the unknown. Back your ideas when nobody believes in the idea. People are accustomed to reject new ideas.

29. Always be your biggest supporter. Have faith in your abilities, always back yourself. Whatever happens, always be your biggest supporter. *This is the Golden power.*

30. Take consistent imperfect action. Do not wait for perfection, strive for excellence.

31. Start using the tool of creative visualisation.

32. Add Music to your life. It makes us more happy and more focussed.

33. WIN: Live by the "WIN" principal, always do what is important now. Make it your *brain tattoo.*

34. Learn to enjoy while you are chasing your goals.

35. Be committed to cheerfulness and playfulness every single day.

36. " If you have one eye on the goal, you are left with only one eye to find your way"- Sadhguru.

37. Be committed to enjoy the process of growth and progress.

Jot down your thoughts, as you have finished reading
the entire book:

Reflect on new insights you have gained and apply them to
your life situation.

May I ask you for a small Favor?

At the outset, I want to give you a big thanks for taking out time to read this book. You could have chosen any other book, but you took mine, and I totally appreciate this.

I believe you got many actionable insights that will have a positive impact on your day-to-day life.

Can I ask for 60 seconds more of your time?

I'd love if you could leave a review about the book. Reviews may not matter to big-name authors; but they're a tremendous help for authors like me, who are taking the road less travelled and trying to make a career in writing. They help me grow my readership by encouraging folks to take a chance on my books.

To put it straight–**reviews are the lifeblood for any author.**

Please leave your review by clicking the below link, it will directly lead you to the book review page.

DIRECT REVIEW LINK FOR "LET IT BE INCOMPLETE"

It will just take less than a minute of your time, but will help me reach out to more people, so please leave your review.

Thanks for your support in my work. And I'd love to see your review.

Bibliography

1. Duckworth, Angela. Grit: The Power of Passion and Perseverance. Scribner, 2016.

   - Source for the research on grit and its impact on achieving long-term goals.

2. Dweck, Carol S. Mindset: The New Psychology of Success. Ballantine Books, 2006.

   - Research on growth mindset and its role in overcoming challenges.

3. Baumeister, Roy F., and Tierney, John. Willpower: Rediscovering the Greatest Human Strength. Penguin Books, 2011.

   - A key source for the chapter on delayed gratification and self-control.

4. Mischel, Walter. The Marshmallow Test: Understanding Self-Control and How to Master It. Back Bay Books, 2015.

   - The source of the famous Marshmallow Test study on delayed gratification and its importance.

5. Clear, James. Atomic Habits: An Easy & Proven Way to Build Good Habits & Break Bad Ones. Avery, 2018.

   - Research and insights on the power of small wins and habit formation.

6. Brown, Brené. The Gifts of Imperfection: Let Go of Who You Think You're Supposed to Be and Embrace Who You Are. Hazelden Publishing, 2010.

   - Ideas on vulnerability, embracing imperfection, and living wholeheartedly.

7. Seligman, Martin E.P. Flourish: A Visionary New Understanding of Happiness and Well-being. Atria Books, 2011.

   - Used for discussions on positive psychology, well-being, and the power of progress over perfection.

8. Kabat-Zinn, Jon. Wherever You Go, There You Are: Mindfulness Meditation in Everyday Life. Hachette Books, 1994.

   - Insights on mindfulness and living in the present moment, aligned with the message of progress over perfection.

9. Thaler, Richard H., and Sunstein, Cass R. Nudge: Improving Decisions About Health, Wealth, and Happiness. Penguin Books, 2008.

   - Research supporting the concept of choice architecture and small behavioral changes leading to big outcomes.

10. Covey, Stephen R. The 7 Habits of Highly Effective People: Powerful Lessons in Personal Change. Free Press, 1989.

   - Referenced for practical insights into goal setting and personal growth strategies.

11. Robinson, Ken. The Element: How Finding Your Passion Changes Everything. Penguin Books, 2009.

   - Story references and ideas on the importance of creativity and passion in achieving personal fulfillment.

12. Pressfield, Steven. The War of Art: Break Through the Blocks and Win Your Inner Creative Battles. Black Irish Entertainment LLC, 2002.

   - Discussed for its emphasis on overcoming resistance, procrastination, and perfectionism in creative work.

13. Tolle, Eckhart. The Power of Now: A Guide to Spiritual Enlightenment. New World Library, 1997.

   - Concepts about living in the present and letting go of the obsession with outcomes.

14. James, William. The Principles of Psychology. Henry Holt, 1890.

   - Early foundational research on psychology, referenced in relation to decision-making and human behavior.

15. Mlodinow, Leonard. Subliminal: How Your Unconscious Mind Rules Your Behavior. Vintage, 2013.

   - For the chapter on limiting beliefs and how subconscious patterns influence behavior.

16. Csikszentmihalyi, Mihaly. Flow: The Psychology of Optimal Experience. Harper & Row, 1990.

   - Referenced for the concept of "flow" and how embracing progress leads to a fulfilling life.

17. Brown, Daniel. The Science of Self-Control: 24 Techniques to Help You Stick to Your Goals. Hay House, 2022.

   - Supporting material for the sections on self-regulation, delayed gratification, and overcoming procrastination.

18. Simmons, Laurence. Unfinished: Thoughts Left Visible. The Metropolitan Museum of Art, 2016.

   - Source for the exploration of incomplete works and their beauty, such as Beethoven's Unfinished Symphony.

19. James, Simon. The Little Book of Kaizen: A Simple Way to Boost Your Productivity. HarperCollins, 2020.

   - Source for your chapter on the power of Kaizen and small continuous improvements.

20. Emoto, Masaru. The Hidden Messages in Water. Beyond Words, 2004.

Inspiration because small, often imperceptible changes can have profound effects, aligned with the theme of small wins. While researching these questions to bring clarity to our "why," the following resources were referenced:

1. **Core Values**–*The Seven Habits of Highly Effective People* by Stephen Covey

2. **Peak Performance**–The work of Mihaly Csikszentmihalyi

3. **Feedback from Others**–Johari Window model

4. **Fear of Failure**–Self-Determination Theory by Edward Deci and Richard Ryan

5. **Legacy and Mortality**–*Man's Search for Meaning* by Viktor Frankl

Thank you

Love + Respect + Gratitude

Pushpendra Singh